50 Russian Ramen Recipes for Home

By: Kelly Johnson

Table of Contents

- Classic Beef Ramen
- Chicken and Mushroom Ramen
- Shrimp Ramen with Garlic Butter
- Vegetarian Ramen with Tofu and Bok Choy
- Pork Belly Ramen
- Spicy Kimchi Ramen
- Salmon Ramen with Miso Broth
- Duck Ramen with Soy Sauce Egg
- Lamb Ramen with Cumin and Coriander
- Vegan Ramen with Seared Tempeh
- Beef and Kimchi Ramen
- Chicken Ramen with Corn and Bean Sprouts
- Mushroom Ramen with Truffle Oil
- Pork Ramen with Pickled Vegetables
- Spicy Sausage Ramen
- Turkey Ramen with Sage and Thyme
- Seafood Ramen with Clams and Shrimp
- Vegan Ramen with Shiitake Mushrooms
- Beef Short Rib Ramen
- Chicken Ramen with Spinach and Sesame
- Pork Ramen with Bamboo Shoots
- Tofu Ramen with Peanut Sauce
- Duck Confit Ramen
- Beef Brisket Ramen
- Vegetarian Ramen with Roasted Vegetables
- Chicken Ramen with Nori and Scallions
- Pork Ramen with Kimchi and Egg
- Beef Ramen with Ginger and Garlic
- Salmon Ramen with Wakame and Soy
- Lamb Ramen with Harissa
- Vegan Ramen with Spicy Miso Broth
- Chicken Ramen with Shiitake and Mirin
- Pork Ramen with Black Garlic Oil
- Beef Ramen with Sichuan Peppercorns
- Shrimp Ramen with Lemongrass and Coconut Milk

- Vegan Ramen with Crispy Tofu
- Duck Ramen with Hoisin Sauce
- Beef Ramen with Ponzu and Mirin
- Chicken Ramen with Soy-Marinated Egg
- Pork Ramen with Spicy Bean Paste
- Turkey Ramen with Sage Butter
- Seafood Ramen with Thai Curry Broth
- Vegan Ramen with Kimchi and Sesame
- Beef Ramen with Mushrooms and Soy
- Chicken Ramen with Charred Corn
- Pork Ramen with Ramson Pesto
- Duck Ramen with Five-Spice Powder
- Beef Ramen with Caramelized Onions
- Chicken Ramen with Lemongrass and Galangal
- Vegetarian Ramen with Crispy Shallots

Classic Beef Ramen

Ingredients:

- 2 packs of ramen noodles (discard seasoning packets)
- 1 lb beef sirloin or flank steak, thinly sliced
- 6 cups beef broth
- 4 cloves garlic, minced
- 1-inch piece of ginger, grated
- 2 tbsp soy sauce
- 1 tbsp mirin (Japanese sweet rice wine)
- 1 tbsp sake (Japanese rice wine) (optional)
- 1 tbsp sesame oil
- 1 tbsp vegetable oil
- 2 green onions, chopped (white and green parts separated)
- 2 eggs
- Salt and pepper, to taste
- Toppings: sliced mushrooms, spinach, bamboo shoots, nori (seaweed), corn kernels, sesame seeds

Instructions:

1. **Marinate the Beef:**
   - In a bowl, combine the sliced beef with minced garlic, grated ginger, soy sauce, mirin, and sake (if using). Let it marinate for at least 15-20 minutes.
2. **Prepare the Broth:**
   - Heat vegetable oil in a large pot over medium heat. Add the white parts of the green onions and sauté for 1-2 minutes until fragrant.
   - Pour in the beef broth and bring to a simmer. Let it simmer for about 10 minutes to allow the flavors to meld together.
3. **Cook the Eggs:**
   - While the broth is simmering, bring a separate pot of water to a boil. Carefully add the eggs and boil for 6-7 minutes for soft-boiled eggs (adjust timing for desired yolk consistency). Remove the eggs and place them in cold water to stop cooking. Once cooled, peel and set aside.
4. **Cook the Beef:**
   - In a separate pan, heat sesame oil over medium-high heat. Add the marinated beef slices (reserving the marinade) and stir-fry for 2-3 minutes until browned and cooked through. Remove the beef from the pan and set aside.
5. **Assemble the Ramen:**
   - Bring a pot of water to a boil and cook the ramen noodles according to the package instructions. Drain and rinse under cold water to stop cooking. Divide the noodles among serving bowls.
6. **Finish the Broth:**

- Add the reserved marinade to the simmering broth. Taste and adjust seasoning with salt and pepper if needed.

7. **Serve:**
    - Pour the hot broth over the noodles in each bowl. Arrange the cooked beef slices on top. Slice the boiled eggs in half and add them to each bowl. Garnish with desired toppings such as sliced mushrooms, spinach, bamboo shoots, nori, corn kernels, sesame seeds, and the green parts of the chopped green onions.
8. **Enjoy!**
    - Serve hot and enjoy your classic beef ramen!

This recipe serves 2-4 people depending on portion sizes. Adjust the ingredients accordingly for larger servings.

Chicken and Mushroom Ramen

Ingredients:

- 2 packs of ramen noodles (discard seasoning packets)
- 1 lb boneless, skinless chicken thighs or breasts, thinly sliced
- 6 cups chicken broth
- 1 cup sliced mushrooms (shiitake, cremini, or your choice)
- 4 cloves garlic, minced
- 1-inch piece of ginger, grated
- 2 tbsp soy sauce
- 1 tbsp mirin (Japanese sweet rice wine)
- 1 tbsp sake (Japanese rice wine) (optional)
- 1 tbsp sesame oil
- 1 tbsp vegetable oil
- 2 green onions, chopped (white and green parts separated)
- 2 eggs
- Salt and pepper, to taste
- Toppings: sliced bamboo shoots, spinach, nori (seaweed), corn kernels, sesame seeds

Instructions:

1. **Marinate the Chicken:**
   - In a bowl, combine the sliced chicken with minced garlic, grated ginger, soy sauce, mirin, and sake (if using). Let it marinate for at least 15-20 minutes.
2. **Prepare the Broth:**
   - Heat vegetable oil in a large pot over medium heat. Add the white parts of the green onions and sauté for 1-2 minutes until fragrant.
   - Add the sliced mushrooms and continue to sauté for another 2-3 minutes until mushrooms are softened.
3. **Cook the Chicken:**
   - Push the mushrooms and onions to the side of the pot. Add the marinated chicken to the center and cook for 5-6 minutes until chicken is cooked through.
4. **Add Broth:**
   - Pour in the chicken broth and bring to a simmer. Let it simmer for about 10 minutes to allow the flavors to meld together.
5. **Cook the Eggs:**
   - While the broth is simmering, bring a separate pot of water to a boil. Carefully add the eggs and boil for 6-7 minutes for soft-boiled eggs (adjust timing for desired yolk consistency). Remove the eggs and place them in cold water to stop cooking. Once cooled, peel and set aside.
6. **Prepare Ramen Noodles:**

- In the meantime, bring another pot of water to a boil and cook the ramen noodles according to the package instructions. Drain and rinse under cold water to stop cooking. Divide the noodles among serving bowls.
7. **Finish the Ramen:**
    - Once the broth is ready, taste and adjust seasoning with salt and pepper if needed. Stir in sesame oil.
8. **Serve:**
    - Pour the hot broth over the noodles in each bowl. Arrange the cooked chicken slices and mushrooms on top. Slice the boiled eggs in half and add them to each bowl. Garnish with desired toppings such as sliced bamboo shoots, spinach, nori, corn kernels, sesame seeds, and the green parts of the chopped green onions.
9. **Enjoy!**
    - Serve hot and enjoy your delicious chicken and mushroom ramen!

This recipe serves 2-4 people depending on portion sizes. Adjust the ingredients accordingly for larger servings.

Shrimp Ramen with Garlic Butter

Ingredients:

- 2 packs of ramen noodles (discard seasoning packets)
- 1 lb large shrimp, peeled and deveined
- 6 cups chicken broth or seafood broth
- 4 cloves garlic, minced
- 1-inch piece of ginger, grated
- 2 tbsp soy sauce
- 1 tbsp mirin (Japanese sweet rice wine)
- 1 tbsp sake (Japanese rice wine) (optional)
- 1 tbsp sesame oil
- 1 tbsp vegetable oil
- 2 tbsp unsalted butter
- 2 green onions, chopped (white and green parts separated)
- 2 eggs
- Salt and pepper, to taste
- Toppings: sliced mushrooms, spinach, bamboo shoots, nori (seaweed), corn kernels, sesame seeds

Instructions:

1. **Prepare the Shrimp:**
    - In a bowl, combine the shrimp with minced garlic, grated ginger, soy sauce, mirin, and sake (if using). Let it marinate for about 10 minutes.
2. **Cook the Eggs:**
    - While the shrimp is marinating, bring a separate pot of water to a boil. Carefully add the eggs and boil for 6-7 minutes for soft-boiled eggs (adjust timing for desired yolk consistency). Remove the eggs and place them in cold water to stop cooking. Once cooled, peel and set aside.
3. **Prepare Ramen Noodles:**
    - In the meantime, bring another pot of water to a boil and cook the ramen noodles according to the package instructions. Drain and rinse under cold water to stop cooking. Divide the noodles among serving bowls.
4. **Cook the Shrimp:**
    - Heat vegetable oil in a large skillet over medium-high heat. Add the marinated shrimp and cook for 2-3 minutes on each side until shrimp turn pink and opaque. Remove shrimp from the skillet and set aside.
5. **Prepare the Broth:**
    - In the same skillet, melt the butter over medium heat. Add the minced garlic and sauté for 1-2 minutes until fragrant.
6. **Add Broth:**

- Pour in the chicken or seafood broth and bring to a simmer. Let it simmer for about 10 minutes to allow the flavors to meld together. Stir in sesame oil.

7. **Finish the Ramen:**
   - Taste and adjust seasoning with salt and pepper if needed. Stir in half of the chopped green onions.
8. **Serve:**
   - Pour the hot broth over the noodles in each bowl. Arrange the cooked shrimp on top. Slice the boiled eggs in half and add them to each bowl. Garnish with desired toppings such as sliced mushrooms, spinach, bamboo shoots, nori, corn kernels, sesame seeds, and the remaining chopped green onions.
9. **Enjoy!**
   - Serve hot and enjoy your flavorful shrimp ramen with garlic butter!

This recipe serves 2-4 people depending on portion sizes. Adjust the ingredients accordingly for larger servings.

Vegetarian Ramen with Tofu and Bok Choy

Ingredients:

- 2 packs of ramen noodles (discard seasoning packets)
- 1 block firm tofu, drained and cut into cubes
- 6 cups vegetable broth
- 4 cloves garlic, minced
- 1-inch piece of ginger, grated
- 2 tbsp soy sauce
- 1 tbsp mirin (Japanese sweet rice wine)
- 1 tbsp sesame oil
- 1 tbsp vegetable oil
- 2 heads of baby bok choy, chopped
- 2 green onions, chopped (white and green parts separated)
- 2 eggs (optional)
- Salt and pepper, to taste
- Toppings: sliced mushrooms, corn kernels, nori (seaweed), sesame seeds, sliced bamboo shoots

Instructions:

1. **Prepare the Tofu:**
   - Heat vegetable oil in a large skillet over medium-high heat. Add the tofu cubes and cook until golden and crispy on all sides, about 8-10 minutes. Remove tofu from the skillet and set aside.
2. **Cook the Eggs (if using):**
   - While tofu is cooking, bring a separate pot of water to a boil. Carefully add the eggs and boil for 6-7 minutes for soft-boiled eggs (adjust timing for desired yolk consistency). Remove the eggs and place them in cold water to stop cooking. Once cooled, peel and set aside.
3. **Prepare Ramen Noodles:**
   - In the meantime, bring another pot of water to a boil and cook the ramen noodles according to the package instructions. Drain and rinse under cold water to stop cooking. Divide the noodles among serving bowls.
4. **Prepare Broth:**
   - In the same skillet used for tofu, add minced garlic and grated ginger. Sauté for 1-2 minutes until fragrant. Add soy sauce, mirin, and vegetable broth. Bring to a simmer and let it simmer for about 10 minutes to allow the flavors to meld together. Stir in sesame oil.
5. **Add Bok Choy:**
   - Add chopped bok choy to the broth and cook for 2-3 minutes until bok choy is tender-crisp.
6. **Finish Ramen:**

- Taste and adjust seasoning with salt and pepper if needed. Stir in half of the chopped green onions.
7. **Serve:**
    - Pour the hot broth over the noodles in each bowl. Arrange the crispy tofu cubes on top. Slice the boiled eggs in half and add them to each bowl (if using). Garnish with desired toppings such as sliced mushrooms, corn kernels, nori, sesame seeds, bamboo shoots, and the remaining chopped green onions.
8. **Enjoy!**
    - Serve hot and enjoy your delicious vegetarian ramen with tofu and bok choy!

This recipe serves 2-4 people depending on portion sizes. Adjust the ingredients accordingly for larger servings.

Pork Belly Ramen

Ingredients:

- 2 packs of ramen noodles (discard seasoning packets)
- 1 lb pork belly, skin removed and cut into thin slices
- 6 cups pork or chicken broth
- 4 cloves garlic, minced
- 1-inch piece of ginger, sliced
- 2 tbsp soy sauce
- 1 tbsp mirin (Japanese sweet rice wine)
- 1 tbsp sake (Japanese rice wine) (optional)
- 1 tbsp sesame oil
- 1 tbsp vegetable oil
- 2 green onions, chopped (white and green parts separated)
- 2 eggs
- Salt and pepper, to taste
- Toppings: sliced bamboo shoots, spinach, nori (seaweed), corn kernels, sesame seeds

Instructions:

1. **Prepare the Pork Belly:**
    - Heat vegetable oil in a large pot or Dutch oven over medium-high heat. Add the pork belly slices and cook until browned and crispy on both sides, about 3-4 minutes per side. Remove pork belly from the pot and set aside on a plate lined with paper towels to drain excess oil.
2. **Cook the Eggs:**
    - While the pork belly is cooking, bring a separate pot of water to a boil. Carefully add the eggs and boil for 6-7 minutes for soft-boiled eggs (adjust timing for desired yolk consistency). Remove the eggs and place them in cold water to stop cooking. Once cooled, peel and set aside.
3. **Prepare Ramen Noodles:**
    - In the same pot used for pork belly (or a separate pot), bring water to a boil and cook the ramen noodles according to package instructions. Drain and rinse under cold water to stop cooking. Divide the noodles among serving bowls.
4. **Prepare Broth:**
    - In the pot used for cooking pork belly, add minced garlic and sliced ginger. Sauté for 1-2 minutes until fragrant. Add soy sauce, mirin, sake (if using), and pork or chicken broth. Bring to a simmer and let it simmer for about 10 minutes to allow the flavors to meld together. Stir in sesame oil.
5. **Slice Pork Belly:**
    - Once cooled slightly, slice the cooked pork belly into thin strips.
6. **Finish Ramen:**

- Taste and adjust seasoning of the broth with salt and pepper if needed. Stir in half of the chopped green onions.
7. **Serve:**
    - Divide the cooked ramen noodles among serving bowls. Pour the hot broth over the noodles. Arrange the sliced pork belly on top. Slice the boiled eggs in half and add them to each bowl. Garnish with desired toppings such as sliced bamboo shoots, spinach, nori, corn kernels, sesame seeds, and the remaining chopped green onions.
8. **Enjoy!**
    - Serve hot and enjoy your delicious pork belly ramen!

This recipe serves 2-4 people depending on portion sizes. Adjust the ingredients accordingly for larger servings.

Spicy Kimchi Ramen

Ingredients:

- 2 packs of ramen noodles (discard seasoning packets)
- 1 cup kimchi, chopped
- 1 cup kimchi juice (liquid from the kimchi jar)
- 6 cups chicken or vegetable broth
- 1 lb pork belly or pork shoulder, thinly sliced (optional)
- 4 cloves garlic, minced
- 1-inch piece of ginger, grated
- 2 tbsp gochujang (Korean chili paste)
- 1 tbsp soy sauce
- 1 tbsp sesame oil
- 1 tbsp vegetable oil
- 2 green onions, chopped (white and green parts separated)
- 2 eggs
- Salt and pepper, to taste
- Toppings: sliced mushrooms, spinach, bean sprouts, tofu cubes, nori (seaweed), sesame seeds

Instructions:

1. **Prepare the Broth:**
   - Heat vegetable oil in a large pot over medium-high heat. Add minced garlic and grated ginger. Sauté for 1-2 minutes until fragrant.
   - If using pork, add the sliced pork belly or pork shoulder to the pot and cook until browned and cooked through.
2. **Add Kimchi and Kimchi Juice:**
   - Add chopped kimchi to the pot and sauté for 2-3 minutes until slightly softened. Pour in kimchi juice (liquid from the kimchi jar) and stir well.
3. **Make the Spicy Broth:**
   - Stir in gochujang (Korean chili paste) and soy sauce. Mix until well combined.
4. **Add Broth:**
   - Pour in chicken or vegetable broth and bring to a simmer. Let it simmer for about 10-15 minutes to allow the flavors to meld together. Stir in sesame oil.
5. **Cook the Eggs:**
   - While the broth is simmering, bring a separate pot of water to a boil. Carefully add the eggs and boil for 6-7 minutes for soft-boiled eggs (adjust timing for desired yolk consistency). Remove the eggs and place them in cold water to stop cooking. Once cooled, peel and set aside.
6. **Prepare Ramen Noodles:**

- In another pot, bring water to a boil and cook the ramen noodles according to the package instructions. Drain and rinse under cold water to stop cooking. Divide the noodles among serving bowls.
7. **Finish Ramen:**
    - Taste the broth and adjust seasoning with salt and pepper if needed. Stir in half of the chopped green onions.
8. **Serve:**
    - Pour the hot spicy kimchi broth over the noodles in each bowl. Arrange the cooked pork (if using) on top. Slice the boiled eggs in half and add them to each bowl. Garnish with desired toppings such as sliced mushrooms, spinach, bean sprouts, tofu cubes, nori, sesame seeds, and the remaining chopped green onions.
9. **Enjoy!**
    - Serve hot and enjoy your spicy kimchi ramen!

This recipe serves 2-4 people depending on portion sizes. Adjust the ingredients accordingly for larger servings.

Salmon Ramen with Miso Broth

Ingredients:

- 2 packs of ramen noodles (discard seasoning packets)
- 1 lb salmon fillet, skinless
- 6 cups fish or vegetable broth
- 4 tbsp white miso paste
- 1 tbsp soy sauce
- 1 tbsp mirin (Japanese sweet rice wine)
- 1 tbsp sesame oil
- 1 tbsp vegetable oil
- 4 cloves garlic, minced
- 1-inch piece of ginger, grated
- 2 green onions, chopped (white and green parts separated)
- 2 eggs
- Salt and pepper, to taste
- Toppings: sliced shiitake mushrooms, baby spinach, corn kernels, nori (seaweed), sesame seeds

Instructions:

1. **Prepare the Salmon:**
    - Preheat your oven to 400°F (200°C). Place the salmon fillet on a baking sheet lined with parchment paper. Drizzle with a bit of sesame oil and season with salt and pepper. Bake for 12-15 minutes, or until the salmon is cooked through and flakes easily with a fork. Once done, remove from the oven and set aside.
2. **Cook the Eggs:**
    - While the salmon is baking, bring a separate pot of water to a boil. Carefully add the eggs and boil for 6-7 minutes for soft-boiled eggs (adjust timing for desired yolk consistency). Remove the eggs and place them in cold water to stop cooking. Once cooled, peel and set aside.
3. **Prepare Ramen Noodles:**
    - In a large pot, bring water to a boil and cook the ramen noodles according to the package instructions. Drain and rinse under cold water to stop cooking. Divide the noodles among serving bowls.
4. **Make the Miso Broth:**
    - In the same pot used for noodles (or a separate pot), heat vegetable oil over medium heat. Add minced garlic and grated ginger. Sauté for 1-2 minutes until fragrant.
    - Add fish or vegetable broth to the pot. Bring to a gentle simmer.
    - In a small bowl, mix miso paste with a ladleful of hot broth until smooth. Add the miso mixture back into the pot, stirring well to combine. Stir in soy sauce, mirin,

and sesame oil. Simmer for about 5 minutes to blend the flavors together. Taste and adjust seasoning with salt and pepper if needed.
5. **Assemble the Ramen:**
    - Divide the cooked ramen noodles among serving bowls. Ladle the hot miso broth over the noodles.
    - Flake the baked salmon into large chunks and place on top of the noodles and broth.
    - Slice the boiled eggs in half and add them to each bowl. Garnish with desired toppings such as sliced shiitake mushrooms, baby spinach, corn kernels, nori, sesame seeds, and the chopped green parts of the green onions.
6. **Serve and Enjoy!**
    - Serve hot and enjoy your delicious salmon ramen with miso broth!

This recipe serves 2-4 people depending on portion sizes. Adjust the ingredients accordingly for larger servings.

Duck Ramen with Soy Sauce Egg

Ingredients:

- 2 packs of ramen noodles (discard seasoning packets)
- 2 duck breasts
- 6 cups chicken or duck broth
- 4 cloves garlic, minced
- 1-inch piece of ginger, grated
- 2 tbsp soy sauce
- 1 tbsp mirin (Japanese sweet rice wine)
- 1 tbsp sake (Japanese rice wine) (optional)
- 1 tbsp sesame oil
- 1 tbsp vegetable oil
- 2 green onions, chopped (white and green parts separated)
- 4 eggs
- 4 tbsp soy sauce
- 2 tbsp mirin
- 2 tbsp water
- 2 tsp sugar
- Toppings: sliced shiitake mushrooms, baby spinach, bamboo shoots, nori (seaweed), sesame seeds

Instructions:

1. **Marinate the Duck Breast:**
   - In a bowl, combine 2 tbsp soy sauce, 1 tbsp mirin, and 1 tbsp sake (if using). Score the duck breast skin in a crosshatch pattern. Place the duck breasts in the marinade, skin side down, and let marinate for at least 30 minutes (or up to overnight in the refrigerator).
2. **Prepare the Soy Sauce Eggs:**
   - In a small saucepan, combine 4 tbsp soy sauce, 2 tbsp mirin, 2 tbsp water, and 2 tsp sugar. Bring to a simmer over medium heat, stirring until the sugar is dissolved. Remove from heat and let cool.
   - In a separate pot, bring water to a boil. Carefully add the eggs and boil for 7 minutes for medium-boiled eggs. Remove the eggs and place them in cold water to stop cooking. Once cooled, peel the eggs and place them in the soy sauce mixture to marinate for at least 30 minutes (or longer for deeper flavor).
3. **Cook the Duck Breast:**
   - Preheat oven to 400°F (200°C). Heat vegetable oil in an oven-safe skillet over medium-high heat. Remove the duck breasts from the marinade and pat dry with paper towels. Place the duck breasts in the skillet, skin side down, and cook for 3-4 minutes until the skin is crispy and browned. Flip the duck breasts and transfer the skillet to the preheated oven. Roast for 10-12 minutes for

medium-rare or until desired doneness. Remove from the oven and let rest for a few minutes before slicing thinly.
4. **Prepare Ramen Noodles:**
   - In a large pot, bring water to a boil and cook the ramen noodles according to package instructions. Drain and rinse under cold water to stop cooking. Divide the noodles among serving bowls.
5. **Prepare the Broth:**
   - In the same pot used for noodles (or a separate pot), heat sesame oil over medium heat. Add minced garlic and grated ginger. Sauté for 1-2 minutes until fragrant. Add chicken or duck broth to the pot and bring to a simmer. Let it simmer for about 10 minutes to allow the flavors to meld together. Taste and adjust seasoning with soy sauce or salt if needed.
6. **Assemble the Ramen:**
   - Ladle the hot broth over the noodles in each bowl. Arrange the sliced duck breast on top.
   - Slice the soy sauce-marinated eggs in half and add them to each bowl. Garnish with desired toppings such as sliced shiitake mushrooms, baby spinach, bamboo shoots, nori, sesame seeds, and the chopped green parts of the green onions.
7. **Serve and Enjoy!**
   - Serve hot and enjoy your delicious duck ramen with soy sauce egg!

This recipe serves 2-4 people depending on portion sizes. Adjust the ingredients accordingly for larger servings.

Lamb Ramen with Cumin and Coriander

Ingredients:

- 2 packs of ramen noodles (discard seasoning packets)
- 1 lb lamb shoulder or leg, thinly sliced
- 6 cups beef or lamb broth
- 4 cloves garlic, minced
- 1-inch piece of ginger, grated
- 2 tbsp soy sauce
- 1 tbsp mirin (Japanese sweet rice wine)
- 1 tbsp sesame oil
- 1 tbsp vegetable oil
- 1 tbsp ground cumin
- 1 tbsp ground coriander
- 2 green onions, chopped (white and green parts separated)
- 2 eggs
- Salt and pepper, to taste
- Toppings: sliced shiitake mushrooms, baby spinach, bean sprouts, sliced radishes, cilantro leaves, lime wedges

Instructions:

1. **Prepare the Lamb:**
   - In a bowl, combine the sliced lamb with ground cumin, ground coriander, soy sauce, mirin, and grated ginger. Let it marinate for at least 15-20 minutes.
2. **Cook the Eggs:**
   - While the lamb is marinating, bring a separate pot of water to a boil. Carefully add the eggs and boil for 6-7 minutes for soft-boiled eggs (adjust timing for desired yolk consistency). Remove the eggs and place them in cold water to stop cooking. Once cooled, peel and set aside.
3. **Prepare Ramen Noodles:**
   - In a large pot, bring water to a boil and cook the ramen noodles according to the package instructions. Drain and rinse under cold water to stop cooking. Divide the noodles among serving bowls.
4. **Prepare the Broth:**
   - In a large pot or Dutch oven, heat vegetable oil over medium-high heat. Add minced garlic and sauté for 1-2 minutes until fragrant.
   - Add the marinated lamb slices to the pot and cook until browned and cooked through, about 5-6 minutes.
5. **Add Broth:**
   - Pour in beef or lamb broth and bring to a simmer. Let it simmer for about 10 minutes to allow the flavors to meld together. Stir in sesame oil.
6. **Finish Ramen:**

- Taste and adjust seasoning with salt and pepper if needed. Stir in half of the chopped green onions.

7. **Serve:**
    - Divide the cooked ramen noodles among serving bowls. Ladle the hot broth and lamb slices over the noodles.
    - Slice the boiled eggs in half and add them to each bowl. Garnish with desired toppings such as sliced shiitake mushrooms, baby spinach, bean sprouts, sliced radishes, cilantro leaves, lime wedges, and the remaining chopped green onions.

8. **Enjoy!**
    - Serve hot and enjoy your aromatic lamb ramen with cumin and coriander!

This recipe serves 2-4 people depending on portion sizes. Adjust the ingredients accordingly for larger servings.

Vegan Ramen with Seared Tempeh

Ingredients:

- 2 packs of ramen noodles (discard seasoning packets)
- 1 block of tempeh, sliced into thin strips
- 6 cups vegetable broth
- 4 cloves garlic, minced
- 1-inch piece of ginger, grated
- 2 tbsp soy sauce
- 1 tbsp miso paste
- 1 tbsp sesame oil
- 1 tbsp vegetable oil
- 2 green onions, chopped (white and green parts separated)
- 1 tbsp rice vinegar
- 1 tbsp maple syrup or agave syrup
- Toppings: sliced shiitake mushrooms, baby spinach, bean sprouts, nori (seaweed), sliced radishes, sesame seeds

Instructions:

1. **Prepare the Tempeh:**
   - Heat vegetable oil in a large skillet over medium-high heat. Add the tempeh strips and cook until golden and crispy on both sides, about 3-4 minutes per side. Remove tempeh from the skillet and set aside on a plate lined with paper towels to drain excess oil.
2. **Cook the Noodles:**
   - In a large pot, bring water to a boil and cook the ramen noodles according to package instructions. Drain and rinse under cold water to stop cooking. Divide the noodles among serving bowls.
3. **Prepare the Broth:**
   - In the same pot used for noodles (or a separate pot), heat sesame oil over medium heat. Add minced garlic and grated ginger. Sauté for 1-2 minutes until fragrant.
   - Add vegetable broth to the pot and bring to a simmer. Let it simmer for about 5 minutes.
   - In a small bowl, mix together soy sauce, miso paste, rice vinegar, and maple syrup/agave syrup until well combined. Add this mixture to the broth, stirring well to incorporate. Simmer for another 5 minutes to allow the flavors to meld together. Taste and adjust seasoning with soy sauce or salt if needed.
4. **Assemble the Ramen:**
   - Ladle the hot broth over the noodles in each bowl.
   - Arrange the seared tempeh strips on top of the noodles.

- Garnish with desired toppings such as sliced shiitake mushrooms, baby spinach, bean sprouts, sliced radishes, nori, sesame seeds, and the chopped green parts of the green onions.
5. **Serve and Enjoy!**
    - Serve hot and enjoy your comforting vegan ramen with seared tempeh!

This recipe serves 2-4 people depending on portion sizes. Adjust the ingredients accordingly for larger servings.Chicken Ramen with Corn and Bean Sprouts

Beef and Kimchi Ramen

Ingredients:

- 2 packs of ramen noodles (discard seasoning packets)
- 1 lb beef (flank steak or sirloin), thinly sliced
- 1 cup kimchi, chopped
- 1 cup kimchi juice (liquid from the kimchi jar)
- 6 cups beef broth
- 4 cloves garlic, minced
- 1-inch piece of ginger, grated
- 2 tbsp soy sauce
- 1 tbsp sesame oil
- 1 tbsp vegetable oil
- 2 green onions, chopped (white and green parts separated)
- 2 eggs
- Salt and pepper, to taste
- Toppings: sliced shiitake mushrooms, baby spinach, bean sprouts, nori (seaweed), sesame seeds

Instructions:

1. **Prepare the Beef:**
   - Heat vegetable oil in a large pot or Dutch oven over medium-high heat. Add minced garlic and grated ginger. Sauté for 1-2 minutes until fragrant.
   - Add the sliced beef to the pot and cook until browned, about 3-4 minutes.
2. **Cook the Eggs:**
   - While the beef is cooking, bring a separate pot of water to a boil. Carefully add the eggs and boil for 6-7 minutes for soft-boiled eggs (adjust timing for desired yolk consistency). Remove the eggs and place them in cold water to stop cooking. Once cooled, peel and set aside.
3. **Prepare Ramen Noodles:**
   - In the same pot used for beef (or a separate pot), bring water to a boil and cook the ramen noodles according to the package instructions. Drain and rinse under cold water to stop cooking. Divide the noodles among serving bowls.
4. **Prepare the Broth:**
   - Return the pot with beef and garlic to medium heat. Add chopped kimchi and sauté for 2-3 minutes until slightly softened.
   - Pour in kimchi juice (liquid from the kimchi jar) and beef broth. Bring to a simmer and let it simmer for about 10 minutes to allow the flavors to meld together. Stir in soy sauce and sesame oil. Taste and adjust seasoning with salt and pepper if needed.
5. **Assemble the Ramen:**

- Divide the cooked ramen noodles among serving bowls. Ladle the hot broth and beef over the noodles.
- Slice the boiled eggs in half and add them to each bowl. Garnish with desired toppings such as sliced shiitake mushrooms, baby spinach, bean sprouts, nori, sesame seeds, and the chopped green parts of the green onions.

6. **Serve and Enjoy!**
    - Serve hot and enjoy your flavorful beef and kimchi ramen!

This recipe serves 2-4 people depending on portion sizes. Adjust the ingredients accordingly for larger servings.

Chicken Ramen with Corn and Bean Sprouts

Ingredients:

- 2 packs of ramen noodles (discard seasoning packets)
- 2 chicken breasts, thinly sliced
- 6 cups chicken broth
- 1 cup corn kernels (fresh or frozen)
- 1 cup bean sprouts
- 4 cloves garlic, minced
- 1-inch piece of ginger, grated
- 2 tbsp soy sauce
- 1 tbsp sesame oil
- 1 tbsp vegetable oil
- 2 green onions, chopped (white and green parts separated)
- 2 eggs
- Salt and pepper, to taste
- Toppings: sliced shiitake mushrooms, nori (seaweed), sesame seeds, sliced bamboo shoots

Instructions:

1. **Prepare the Chicken:**
    - Heat vegetable oil in a large pot or Dutch oven over medium-high heat. Add minced garlic and grated ginger. Sauté for 1-2 minutes until fragrant.
    - Add the sliced chicken breasts to the pot and cook until browned and cooked through, about 5-6 minutes.
2. **Cook the Eggs:**
    - While the chicken is cooking, bring a separate pot of water to a boil. Carefully add the eggs and boil for 6-7 minutes for soft-boiled eggs (adjust timing for desired yolk consistency). Remove the eggs and place them in cold water to stop cooking. Once cooled, peel and set aside.
3. **Prepare Ramen Noodles:**
    - In the same pot used for chicken (or a separate pot), bring water to a boil and cook the ramen noodles according to the package instructions. Drain and rinse under cold water to stop cooking. Divide the noodles among serving bowls.
4. **Prepare the Broth:**
    - Return the pot with chicken, garlic, and ginger to medium heat. Add chicken broth to the pot and bring to a simmer. Let it simmer for about 5 minutes.
    - Stir in soy sauce and sesame oil. Taste and adjust seasoning with salt and pepper if needed.
5. **Add Corn and Bean Sprouts:**
    - Add corn kernels and bean sprouts to the simmering broth. Cook for another 2-3 minutes until corn is heated through and bean sprouts are tender-crisp.

6. **Assemble the Ramen:**
   - Divide the cooked ramen noodles among serving bowls. Ladle the hot broth, chicken, corn, and bean sprouts over the noodles.
7. **Serve and Garnish:**
   - Slice the boiled eggs in half and add them to each bowl. Garnish with desired toppings such as sliced shiitake mushrooms, nori, sesame seeds, sliced bamboo shoots, and the chopped green parts of the green onions.
8. **Enjoy!**
   - Serve hot and enjoy your delicious chicken ramen with corn and bean sprouts!

This recipe serves 2-4 people depending on portion sizes. Adjust the ingredients accordingly for larger servings.

Mushroom Ramen with Truffle Oil

Ingredients:

- 2 packs of ramen noodles (discard seasoning packets)
- 6 cups vegetable broth
- 1 lb mixed mushrooms (such as shiitake, cremini, and oyster), sliced
- 4 cloves garlic, minced
- 1-inch piece of ginger, grated
- 2 tbsp soy sauce
- 1 tbsp mirin (Japanese sweet rice wine)
- 1 tbsp truffle oil
- 1 tbsp sesame oil
- 1 tbsp vegetable oil
- 2 green onions, chopped (white and green parts separated)
- Salt and pepper, to taste
- Toppings: sliced green onions, nori (seaweed), sesame seeds, soft-boiled egg (optional)

Instructions:

1. **Prepare the Mushrooms:**
    - Heat vegetable oil in a large pot or Dutch oven over medium-high heat. Add minced garlic and grated ginger. Sauté for 1-2 minutes until fragrant.
    - Add the sliced mushrooms to the pot and cook until they release their juices and start to brown, about 5-6 minutes.
2. **Cook the Ramen Noodles:**
    - In the same pot, add vegetable broth and bring to a simmer. Let it simmer for about 10 minutes to allow the flavors to meld together.
3. **Prepare the Broth:**
    - Stir in soy sauce and mirin. Taste and adjust seasoning with salt and pepper if needed. Reduce heat to low and stir in truffle oil and sesame oil.
4. **Cook the Ramen Noodles:**
    - In a separate pot, bring water to a boil and cook the ramen noodles according to the package instructions. Drain and rinse under cold water to stop cooking. Divide the noodles among serving bowls.
5. **Assemble the Ramen:**
    - Ladle the hot mushroom broth over the noodles in each bowl.
    - Top with the sautéed mushrooms.
    - Garnish with sliced green onions, nori, sesame seeds, and the chopped green parts of the green onions.
6. **Optional: Soft-Boiled Egg**
    - If desired, slice a soft-boiled egg in half and add it to each bowl as an additional topping.
7. **Serve and Enjoy!**

- Serve hot and savor the earthy flavors of mushroom ramen with truffle oil!

This recipe serves 2-4 people depending on portion sizes. Adjust the ingredients accordingly for larger servings.

Pork Ramen with Pickled Vegetables

Ingredients:

- 2 packs of ramen noodles (discard seasoning packets)
- 1 lb pork tenderloin or pork shoulder, thinly sliced
- 6 cups pork or chicken broth
- 1 cup pickled vegetables (such as carrots, radishes, cucumbers)
- 4 cloves garlic, minced
- 1-inch piece of ginger, grated
- 2 tbsp soy sauce
- 1 tbsp mirin (Japanese sweet rice wine)
- 1 tbsp sesame oil
- 1 tbsp vegetable oil
- 2 green onions, chopped (white and green parts separated)
- 2 eggs
- Salt and pepper, to taste
- Toppings: sliced bamboo shoots, nori (seaweed), sesame seeds, cilantro leaves

Instructions:

1. **Prepare the Pork:**
    - Heat vegetable oil in a large pot or Dutch oven over medium-high heat. Add minced garlic and grated ginger. Sauté for 1-2 minutes until fragrant.
    - Add the sliced pork to the pot and cook until browned and cooked through, about 4-5 minutes. Remove pork from the pot and set aside.
2. **Cook the Eggs:**
    - While the pork is cooking, bring a separate pot of water to a boil. Carefully add the eggs and boil for 6-7 minutes for soft-boiled eggs (adjust timing for desired yolk consistency). Remove the eggs and place them in cold water to stop cooking. Once cooled, peel and set aside.
3. **Prepare Ramen Noodles:**
    - In the same pot used for pork (or a separate pot), bring water to a boil and cook the ramen noodles according to the package instructions. Drain and rinse under cold water to stop cooking. Divide the noodles among serving bowls.
4. **Prepare the Broth:**
    - In the same pot used for pork (or a separate pot if needed), add pork or chicken broth and bring to a simmer. Stir in soy sauce, mirin, and sesame oil. Let it simmer for about 5 minutes to meld the flavors together. Taste and adjust seasoning with salt and pepper if needed.
5. **Assemble the Ramen:**
    - Divide the cooked ramen noodles among serving bowls. Ladle the hot broth over the noodles.
    - Arrange the cooked pork slices on top of the noodles.

- Slice the boiled eggs in half and add them to each bowl.
6. **Add Pickled Vegetables:**
    - Place a portion of pickled vegetables (such as carrots, radishes, and cucumbers) on one side of each bowl.
7. **Garnish and Serve:**
    - Garnish with sliced bamboo shoots, nori, sesame seeds, and the chopped green parts of the green onions.
    - Optionally, add a few cilantro leaves for freshness.
8. **Enjoy!**
    - Serve hot and enjoy your delicious pork ramen with pickled vegetables!

This recipe serves 2-4 people depending on portion sizes. Adjust the ingredients accordingly for larger servings.

Spicy Sausage Ramen

Ingredients:

- 2 packs of ramen noodles (discard seasoning packets)
- 1 lb spicy sausage (such as chorizo or spicy Italian sausage), casing removed and crumbled
- 6 cups chicken or beef broth
- 4 cloves garlic, minced
- 1-inch piece of ginger, grated
- 2 tbsp soy sauce
- 1 tbsp sesame oil
- 1 tbsp vegetable oil
- 2 green onions, chopped (white and green parts separated)
- 2 eggs
- 1-2 tbsp gochujang (Korean chili paste), adjust to taste
- 1 tbsp sriracha sauce, adjust to taste (optional for extra heat)
- Toppings: sliced shiitake mushrooms, baby spinach, corn kernels, bean sprouts, nori (seaweed), sesame seeds

Instructions:

1. **Cook the Sausage:**
   - Heat vegetable oil in a large pot or Dutch oven over medium-high heat. Add minced garlic and grated ginger. Sauté for 1-2 minutes until fragrant.
   - Add crumbled spicy sausage to the pot and cook until browned and cooked through, breaking up any large chunks with a spoon, about 5-6 minutes.
2. **Cook the Eggs:**
   - While the sausage is cooking, bring a separate pot of water to a boil. Carefully add the eggs and boil for 6-7 minutes for soft-boiled eggs (adjust timing for desired yolk consistency). Remove the eggs and place them in cold water to stop cooking. Once cooled, peel and set aside.
3. **Prepare Ramen Noodles:**
   - In the same pot used for sausage (or a separate pot), bring water to a boil and cook the ramen noodles according to the package instructions. Drain and rinse under cold water to stop cooking. Divide the noodles among serving bowls.
4. **Prepare the Broth:**
   - In the same pot used for sausage (or a separate pot if needed), add chicken or beef broth and bring to a simmer.
   - Stir in soy sauce, sesame oil, gochujang (Korean chili paste), and sriracha sauce (if using). Adjust the amount of gochujang and sriracha to your desired level of spiciness.
   - Let the broth simmer for about 5 minutes to allow the flavors to meld together. Taste and adjust seasoning with soy sauce or salt if needed.

5. **Assemble the Ramen:**
    - Divide the cooked ramen noodles among serving bowls. Ladle the hot spicy broth over the noodles.
    - Arrange the cooked spicy sausage on top of the noodles.
    - Slice the boiled eggs in half and add them to each bowl.
6. **Add Toppings:**
    - Garnish with sliced shiitake mushrooms, baby spinach, corn kernels, bean sprouts, nori, sesame seeds, and the chopped green parts of the green onions.
7. **Serve and Enjoy!**
    - Serve hot and enjoy your spicy sausage ramen!

This recipe serves 2-4 people depending on portion sizes. Adjust the ingredients accordingly for larger servings. Adjust the level of spiciness to your taste preference by varying the amount of gochujang and sriracha sauce.

Turkey Ramen with Sage and Thyme

Ingredients:

- 2 packs of ramen noodles (discard seasoning packets)
- 1 lb ground turkey
- 6 cups turkey or chicken broth
- 4 cloves garlic, minced
- 1-inch piece of ginger, grated
- 1 tbsp soy sauce
- 1 tbsp mirin (Japanese sweet rice wine)
- 1 tbsp sesame oil
- 1 tbsp vegetable oil
- 1 tbsp fresh sage leaves, chopped (or 1 tsp dried sage)
- 1 tbsp fresh thyme leaves (or 1 tsp dried thyme)
- 2 green onions, chopped (white and green parts separated)
- 2 eggs
- Salt and pepper, to taste
- Toppings: sliced shiitake mushrooms, baby spinach, sliced bamboo shoots, nori (seaweed), sesame seeds

Instructions:

1. **Prepare the Ground Turkey:**
    - Heat vegetable oil in a large pot or Dutch oven over medium-high heat. Add minced garlic and grated ginger. Sauté for 1-2 minutes until fragrant.
    - Add ground turkey to the pot and cook until browned and cooked through, breaking up any large chunks with a spoon, about 5-6 minutes.
2. **Cook the Eggs:**
    - While the turkey is cooking, bring a separate pot of water to a boil. Carefully add the eggs and boil for 6-7 minutes for soft-boiled eggs (adjust timing for desired yolk consistency). Remove the eggs and place them in cold water to stop cooking. Once cooled, peel and set aside.
3. **Prepare Ramen Noodles:**
    - In the same pot used for turkey (or a separate pot), bring water to a boil and cook the ramen noodles according to the package instructions. Drain and rinse under cold water to stop cooking. Divide the noodles among serving bowls.
4. **Prepare the Broth:**
    - In the same pot used for turkey (or a separate pot if needed), add turkey or chicken broth and bring to a simmer.
    - Stir in soy sauce, mirin, sesame oil, chopped sage leaves, and thyme leaves. Let the broth simmer for about 5 minutes to allow the flavors to meld together. Taste and adjust seasoning with salt and pepper if needed.
5. **Assemble the Ramen:**

- Divide the cooked ramen noodles among serving bowls. Ladle the hot broth and turkey over the noodles.
- Slice the boiled eggs in half and add them to each bowl.

6. **Add Toppings:**
   - Garnish with sliced shiitake mushrooms, baby spinach, sliced bamboo shoots, nori, sesame seeds, and the chopped green parts of the green onions.

7. **Serve and Enjoy!**
   - Serve hot and enjoy your comforting turkey ramen with sage and thyme!

This recipe serves 2-4 people depending on portion sizes. Adjust the ingredients accordingly for larger servings.

Seafood Ramen with Clams and Shrimp

Ingredients:

- 2 packs of ramen noodles (discard seasoning packets)
- 1 lb shrimp, peeled and deveined
- 1 lb clams (such as littleneck or Manila), scrubbed
- 6 cups seafood or chicken broth
- 4 cloves garlic, minced
- 1-inch piece of ginger, grated
- 2 tbsp soy sauce
- 1 tbsp mirin (Japanese sweet rice wine)
- 1 tbsp sesame oil
- 1 tbsp vegetable oil
- 1 cup sliced shiitake mushrooms
- 1 cup baby bok choy, chopped
- 2 green onions, chopped (white and green parts separated)
- 2 eggs
- Salt and pepper, to taste
- Toppings: sliced nori (seaweed), sesame seeds, cilantro leaves, lime wedges

Instructions:

1. **Prepare the Seafood:**
    - Heat vegetable oil in a large pot or Dutch oven over medium-high heat. Add minced garlic and grated ginger. Sauté for 1-2 minutes until fragrant.
    - Add shrimp to the pot and cook until pink and opaque, about 2-3 minutes. Remove shrimp from the pot and set aside.
    - Add clams to the pot and pour in 1 cup of water. Cover with a lid and cook for 5-7 minutes until clams have opened. Discard any clams that do not open. Remove clams from shells and set aside.
2. **Cook the Eggs:**
    - While seafood is cooking, bring a separate pot of water to a boil. Carefully add the eggs and boil for 6-7 minutes for soft-boiled eggs (adjust timing for desired yolk consistency). Remove the eggs and place them in cold water to stop cooking. Once cooled, peel and set aside.
3. **Prepare Ramen Noodles:**
    - In the same pot used for seafood (or a separate pot), bring water to a boil and cook the ramen noodles according to the package instructions. Drain and rinse under cold water to stop cooking. Divide the noodles among serving bowls.
4. **Prepare the Broth:**
    - In the same pot used for seafood (or a separate pot if needed), add seafood or chicken broth and bring to a simmer.

- Stir in soy sauce, mirin, and sesame oil. Let the broth simmer for about 5 minutes to meld the flavors together. Taste and adjust seasoning with salt and pepper if needed.
5. **Assemble the Ramen:**
    - Divide the cooked ramen noodles among serving bowls. Ladle the hot broth over the noodles.
    - Arrange the cooked shrimp and clams on top of the noodles.
    - Add sliced shiitake mushrooms and chopped baby bok choy to each bowl.
6. **Add Toppings:**
    - Slice the boiled eggs in half and add them to each bowl.
    - Garnish with sliced nori, sesame seeds, cilantro leaves, lime wedges, and the chopped green parts of the green onions.
7. **Serve and Enjoy!**
    - Serve hot and enjoy your flavorful seafood ramen with clams and shrimp!

This recipe serves 2-4 people depending on portion sizes. Adjust the ingredients accordingly for larger servings.

Vegan Ramen with Shiitake Mushrooms

Ingredients:

- 2 packs of ramen noodles (discard seasoning packets)
- 6 cups vegetable broth
- 1 cup sliced shiitake mushrooms
- 4 cloves garlic, minced
- 1-inch piece of ginger, grated
- 2 tbsp soy sauce (or tamari for gluten-free)
- 1 tbsp miso paste
- 1 tbsp sesame oil
- 1 tbsp vegetable oil
- 2 green onions, chopped (white and green parts separated)
- 1 tbsp rice vinegar
- 1 tbsp maple syrup or agave syrup
- Toppings: baby spinach, bean sprouts, sliced bamboo shoots, nori (seaweed), sesame seeds

Instructions:

1. **Prepare the Shiitake Mushrooms:**
    - Heat vegetable oil in a large pot or Dutch oven over medium-high heat. Add minced garlic and grated ginger. Sauté for 1-2 minutes until fragrant.
    - Add sliced shiitake mushrooms to the pot and cook until they start to brown and release their juices, about 5-6 minutes.
2. **Prepare Ramen Noodles:**
    - In the same pot with mushrooms (or a separate pot), bring water to a boil and cook the ramen noodles according to the package instructions. Drain and rinse under cold water to stop cooking. Divide the noodles among serving bowls.
3. **Prepare the Broth:**
    - In the same pot used for mushrooms (or a separate pot if needed), add vegetable broth and bring to a simmer.
    - In a small bowl, mix together soy sauce (or tamari), miso paste, rice vinegar, and maple syrup/agave syrup until well combined. Add this mixture to the simmering broth.
    - Stir in sesame oil and let the broth simmer for another 5 minutes to allow the flavors to meld together. Taste and adjust seasoning with soy sauce or salt if needed.
4. **Assemble the Ramen:**
    - Divide the cooked ramen noodles among serving bowls.
    - Ladle the hot broth and mushrooms over the noodles.
    - Add baby spinach, bean sprouts, and sliced bamboo shoots to each bowl.
5. **Garnish and Serve:**

- Garnish with sliced nori, sesame seeds, and the chopped green parts of the green onions.
6. **Enjoy!**
    - Serve hot and enjoy your comforting vegan ramen with shiitake mushrooms!

This recipe serves 2-4 people depending on portion sizes. Adjust the ingredients accordingly for larger servings.

Beef Short Rib Ramen

Ingredients:

- 2 lbs beef short ribs
- 2 packs of ramen noodles (discard seasoning packets)
- 8 cups beef broth
- 4 cloves garlic, minced
- 1-inch piece of ginger, sliced
- 2 tbsp soy sauce
- 1 tbsp mirin (Japanese sweet rice wine)
- 1 tbsp sake (optional)
- 1 tbsp miso paste
- 1 tbsp sesame oil
- 1 tbsp vegetable oil
- 2 green onions, chopped (white and green parts separated)
- 1 tbsp rice vinegar
- 1 tbsp brown sugar (optional, for sweetness)
- Toppings: baby spinach, bamboo shoots, nori (seaweed), soft-boiled eggs, sliced shiitake mushrooms, sliced radishes, sesame seeds

Instructions:

1. **Prepare the Beef Short Ribs:**
   - Heat vegetable oil in a large pot or Dutch oven over medium-high heat. Add the beef short ribs and sear on all sides until browned, about 3-4 minutes per side. Remove the ribs and set aside.
2. **Make the Broth:**
   - In the same pot, add garlic, ginger, and the white parts of the green onions. Sauté for 1-2 minutes until fragrant.
   - Add beef broth, soy sauce, mirin, sake (if using), miso paste, sesame oil, rice vinegar, and brown sugar (if using). Stir well to combine.
   - Return the beef short ribs to the pot. Bring the broth to a boil, then reduce the heat to low. Cover and simmer for 2.5 to 3 hours, or until the beef short ribs are tender and easily pull apart.
3. **Prepare the Ramen Noodles:**
   - While the beef short ribs are simmering, prepare the ramen noodles according to the package instructions. Drain and rinse under cold water to stop cooking. Set aside.
4. **Prepare Toppings:**
   - Prepare any toppings you'd like to use, such as slicing bamboo shoots, preparing soft-boiled eggs, slicing shiitake mushrooms, etc.
5. **Finish the Dish:**

- Once the beef short ribs are tender, remove them from the broth and shred the meat using two forks. Discard any bones and excess fat.
- Strain the broth to remove the garlic, ginger, and any solids, leaving a clear broth.

6. **Assemble the Ramen Bowls:**
    - Divide the cooked ramen noodles among serving bowls.
    - Ladle the hot beef short rib broth over the noodles.
    - Add shredded beef short rib meat to each bowl.
7. **Garnish and Serve:**
    - Garnish each bowl with baby spinach, bamboo shoots, nori, sliced shiitake mushrooms, sliced radishes, sesame seeds, and the green parts of the green onions.
8. **Enjoy!**
    - Serve hot and enjoy your hearty beef short rib ramen!

This recipe serves 4-6 people depending on portion sizes. Adjust the ingredients accordingly for larger or smaller servings.

Chicken Ramen with Spinach and Sesame

Ingredients:

- 2 packs of ramen noodles (discard seasoning packets)
- 2 boneless, skinless chicken breasts, thinly sliced
- 6 cups chicken broth
- 4 cups baby spinach leaves
- 4 cloves garlic, minced
- 1-inch piece of ginger, grated
- 2 tbsp soy sauce (or tamari for gluten-free)
- 1 tbsp sesame oil
- 1 tbsp vegetable oil
- 1 tbsp rice vinegar
- 1 tbsp honey or brown sugar
- 2 green onions, chopped (white and green parts separated)
- 1 tbsp sesame seeds, for garnish
- Salt and pepper, to taste

Instructions:

1. **Prepare the Chicken:**
    - Heat vegetable oil in a large pot or Dutch oven over medium-high heat. Add minced garlic and grated ginger. Sauté for 1-2 minutes until fragrant.
    - Add sliced chicken breasts to the pot and cook until browned and cooked through, about 5-6 minutes. Remove chicken from the pot and set aside.
2. **Prepare Ramen Noodles:**
    - In the same pot (or a separate pot), bring water to a boil and cook the ramen noodles according to the package instructions. Drain and rinse under cold water to stop cooking. Divide the noodles among serving bowls.
3. **Make the Broth:**
    - In the same pot used for chicken (or a separate pot if needed), add chicken broth and bring to a simmer.
    - Stir in soy sauce, sesame oil, rice vinegar, and honey or brown sugar. Let the broth simmer for about 5 minutes to allow the flavors to meld together. Taste and adjust seasoning with salt and pepper if needed.
4. **Assemble the Ramen Bowls:**
    - Divide the cooked ramen noodles among serving bowls.
    - Add baby spinach leaves to each bowl.
5. **Finish and Serve:**
    - Ladle the hot broth over the noodles and spinach.
    - Arrange the cooked chicken slices on top.
    - Garnish with chopped green onions and sesame seeds.
6. **Enjoy!**

- Serve hot and enjoy your delicious chicken ramen with spinach and sesame!

This recipe serves 2-4 people depending on portion sizes. Adjust the ingredients accordingly for larger servings. It's a comforting and nutritious dish that's perfect for any time of the year.

Pork Ramen with Bamboo Shoots

Ingredients:

- 2 packs of ramen noodles (discard seasoning packets)
- 1 lb pork loin or pork shoulder, thinly sliced
- 6 cups pork or chicken broth
- 1 cup sliced bamboo shoots (canned or fresh)
- 4 cloves garlic, minced
- 1-inch piece of ginger, grated
- 2 tbsp soy sauce
- 1 tbsp mirin (Japanese sweet rice wine)
- 1 tbsp sesame oil
- 1 tbsp vegetable oil
- 2 green onions, chopped (white and green parts separated)
- 2 eggs
- Salt and pepper, to taste
- Toppings: sliced shiitake mushrooms, baby spinach, nori (seaweed), sesame seeds

Instructions:

1. **Prepare the Pork:**
    - Heat vegetable oil in a large pot or Dutch oven over medium-high heat. Add minced garlic and grated ginger. Sauté for 1-2 minutes until fragrant.
    - Add sliced pork to the pot and cook until browned and cooked through, about 5-6 minutes. Remove pork from the pot and set aside.
2. **Cook the Eggs:**
    - While the pork is cooking, bring a separate pot of water to a boil. Carefully add the eggs and boil for 6-7 minutes for soft-boiled eggs (adjust timing for desired yolk consistency). Remove the eggs and place them in cold water to stop cooking. Once cooled, peel and set aside.
3. **Prepare Ramen Noodles:**
    - In the same pot used for pork (or a separate pot), bring water to a boil and cook the ramen noodles according to the package instructions. Drain and rinse under cold water to stop cooking. Divide the noodles among serving bowls.
4. **Prepare the Broth:**
    - In the same pot used for pork (or a separate pot if needed), add pork or chicken broth and bring to a simmer.
    - Stir in soy sauce, mirin, and sesame oil. Let the broth simmer for about 5 minutes to allow the flavors to meld together. Taste and adjust seasoning with salt and pepper if needed.
5. **Assemble the Ramen:**
    - Divide the cooked ramen noodles among serving bowls. Ladle the hot broth over the noodles.

- Arrange the cooked pork slices and bamboo shoots on top of the noodles.
6. **Add Toppings:**
    - Slice the boiled eggs in half and add them to each bowl.
    - Garnish with sliced shiitake mushrooms, baby spinach, nori, sesame seeds, and the chopped green parts of the green onions.
7. **Serve and Enjoy!**
    - Serve hot and enjoy your flavorful pork ramen with bamboo shoots!

This recipe serves 2-4 people depending on portion sizes. Adjust the ingredients accordingly for larger servings.

Tofu Ramen with Peanut Sauce

Ingredients:

- 2 packs of ramen noodles (discard seasoning packets)
- 1 block (14 oz) firm tofu, cut into cubes
- 6 cups vegetable broth
- 1/3 cup creamy peanut butter
- 2 tbsp soy sauce (or tamari for gluten-free)
- 1 tbsp sesame oil
- 1 tbsp rice vinegar
- 1 tbsp maple syrup or honey
- 2 cloves garlic, minced
- 1-inch piece of ginger, grated
- 1 tbsp vegetable oil
- 2 green onions, chopped (white and green parts separated)
- Crushed peanuts, for garnish (optional)
- Sriracha or chili flakes, for garnish (optional)
- Fresh cilantro leaves, for garnish (optional)

Instructions:

1. **Prepare the Tofu:**
    - Heat vegetable oil in a large skillet over medium-high heat. Add tofu cubes and cook until golden and crispy on all sides, about 8-10 minutes. Remove tofu from skillet and set aside.
2. **Make the Peanut Sauce:**
    - In a small bowl, whisk together peanut butter, soy sauce, sesame oil, rice vinegar, maple syrup (or honey), minced garlic, and grated ginger until smooth. Set aside.
3. **Prepare Ramen Noodles:**
    - In a large pot, bring water to a boil and cook the ramen noodles according to the package instructions. Drain and rinse under cold water to stop cooking. Divide the noodles among serving bowls.
4. **Prepare the Broth:**
    - In the same pot used for noodles (or a separate pot if needed), add vegetable broth and bring to a simmer.
    - Stir in the prepared peanut sauce until well combined. Let the broth simmer for about 5 minutes to allow the flavors to meld together. Taste and adjust seasoning if needed.
5. **Assemble the Ramen Bowls:**
    - Divide the cooked ramen noodles among serving bowls.
    - Ladle the hot peanut broth over the noodles.
6. **Add Toppings:**

        - Arrange the crispy tofu cubes on top of each bowl.
        - Garnish with chopped green onions, crushed peanuts (if using), and a drizzle of sriracha or chili flakes for heat (if desired).
        - Optionally, garnish with fresh cilantro leaves for added freshness.
7. **Serve and Enjoy!**
        - Serve hot and enjoy your delicious tofu ramen with peanut sauce!

This recipe serves 2-4 people depending on portion sizes. Adjust the ingredients accordingly for larger servings. It's a satisfying and flavorful vegan dish that's perfect for a comforting meal.

Duck Confit Ramen

Ingredients:

For the Duck Confit:

- 2 duck legs, preferably already confit (or you can confit them yourself)
- Salt and pepper, to taste
- 2 tbsp duck fat (if not already confited)

For the Ramen:

- 2 packs of ramen noodles (discard seasoning packets)
- 6 cups chicken or duck broth
- 4 cloves garlic, minced
- 1-inch piece of ginger, grated
- 2 tbsp soy sauce
- 1 tbsp mirin (Japanese sweet rice wine)
- 1 tbsp sake (optional)
- 1 tbsp sesame oil
- 1 tbsp vegetable oil
- 2 green onions, chopped (white and green parts separated)
- 2 eggs, soft-boiled
- 1 cup baby spinach
- 1/2 cup sliced bamboo shoots (canned or fresh)
- Nori (seaweed), sliced into strips, for garnish
- Sesame seeds, for garnish

Instructions:

1. **Prepare the Duck Confit (if not already confited):**
    - Preheat your oven to 300°F (150°C).
    - Pat the duck legs dry with paper towels and season generously with salt and pepper.
    - Heat duck fat in an oven-safe skillet over medium-high heat. Once hot, add the duck legs, skin-side down, and cook for 5-6 minutes until golden brown. Flip and cook for another 5 minutes.
    - Transfer the skillet to the preheated oven and cook for 2-2.5 hours, until the meat is very tender and easily pulls away from the bone. Remove from oven and set aside.
2. **Prepare the Ramen Noodles:**
    - In a large pot, bring water to a boil and cook the ramen noodles according to the package instructions. Drain and rinse under cold water to stop cooking. Divide the noodles among serving bowls.
3. **Prepare the Broth:**

- In a large pot or Dutch oven, heat vegetable oil over medium heat. Add minced garlic and grated ginger, sauté for 1-2 minutes until fragrant.
- Pour in chicken or duck broth, soy sauce, mirin, sake (if using), and sesame oil. Bring to a simmer and let it cook for 5 minutes to allow the flavors to meld together. Taste and adjust seasoning if needed.

4. **Assemble the Ramen Bowls:**
   - Divide the cooked ramen noodles among serving bowls.
   - Ladle the hot broth over the noodles.
5. **Prepare the Duck Confit:**
   - Remove the duck meat from the bones of the confit legs and shred into bite-sized pieces.
6. **Finish and Serve:**
   - Divide the shredded duck confit, baby spinach, and bamboo shoots among the serving bowls.
   - Slice the soft-boiled eggs in half and add them to each bowl.
   - Garnish with chopped green onions, nori strips, and sesame seeds.
7. **Enjoy!**
   - Serve hot and enjoy your luxurious Duck Confit Ramen!

This recipe serves 2-4 people depending on portion sizes. Adjust the ingredients accordingly for larger servings. It's a hearty and flavorful dish that will surely impress your guests or family members!

Beef Brisket Ramen

Ingredients:

For the Beef Brisket:

- 1 lb beef brisket
- Salt and pepper, to taste
- 1 tbsp vegetable oil
- 4 cups beef broth
- 2 cups water
- 2 cloves garlic, minced
- 1-inch piece of ginger, grated
- 2 tbsp soy sauce
- 1 tbsp mirin (Japanese sweet rice wine)
- 1 tbsp sake (optional)
- 1 tbsp brown sugar
- 1 star anise (optional)
- 2 green onions, chopped (white and green parts separated)

For the Ramen:

- 2 packs of ramen noodles (discard seasoning packets)
- Baby spinach or bok choy, chopped (optional)
- Soft-boiled eggs, halved
- Sliced bamboo shoots (canned or fresh)
- Nori (seaweed), sliced into strips
- Sesame seeds, for garnish

Instructions:

1. **Prepare the Beef Brisket:**
   - Season the beef brisket generously with salt and pepper.
   - Heat vegetable oil in a large pot or Dutch oven over medium-high heat. Sear the beef brisket on all sides until browned, about 3-4 minutes per side.
   - Add minced garlic and grated ginger to the pot and sauté for 1-2 minutes until fragrant.
   - Pour in beef broth, water, soy sauce, mirin, sake (if using), brown sugar, star anise (if using), and the white parts of the green onions. Bring to a boil.
   - Reduce heat to low, cover, and simmer for 2.5 to 3 hours, or until the beef brisket is tender and easily pulls apart with a fork.
2. **Prepare the Ramen Noodles:**
   - In a separate pot, bring water to a boil and cook the ramen noodles according to the package instructions. Drain and rinse under cold water to stop cooking. Divide the noodles among serving bowls.

3. **Assemble the Ramen Bowls:**
    - Remove the beef brisket from the pot and shred it into bite-sized pieces.
    - Strain the broth to remove solids, leaving a clear broth.
    - Divide the shredded beef brisket among serving bowls.
4. **Finish and Serve:**
    - Ladle the hot broth over the beef brisket and noodles in each bowl.
    - Add baby spinach or bok choy (if using), soft-boiled eggs, sliced bamboo shoots, and nori strips to each bowl.
    - Garnish with chopped green onions and sesame seeds.
5. **Enjoy!**
    - Serve hot and enjoy your comforting Beef Brisket Ramen!

This recipe serves 4 people. Adjust the ingredients accordingly for larger or smaller servings. It's a hearty and flavorful dish that's perfect for a cozy meal.

Vegetarian Ramen with Roasted Vegetables

Ingredients:

For the Roasted Vegetables:

- 2 cups mixed vegetables, such as bell peppers, zucchini, carrots, and broccoli, cut into bite-sized pieces
- 2 tbsp olive oil
- Salt and pepper, to taste
- 1 tsp garlic powder
- 1 tsp paprika

For the Ramen:

- 2 packs of ramen noodles (discard seasoning packets)
- 6 cups vegetable broth
- 4 cloves garlic, minced
- 1-inch piece of ginger, grated
- 2 tbsp soy sauce (or tamari for gluten-free)
- 1 tbsp miso paste
- 1 tbsp sesame oil
- 1 tbsp vegetable oil
- 2 green onions, chopped (white and green parts separated)
- 1 tbsp rice vinegar
- 1 tbsp maple syrup or agave syrup
- Toppings: sliced mushrooms (shiitake or cremini), baby spinach, sliced bamboo shoots, nori (seaweed), sesame seeds

Instructions:

1. **Roast the Vegetables:**
    - Preheat your oven to 400°F (200°C).
    - Toss the mixed vegetables with olive oil, salt, pepper, garlic powder, and paprika on a baking sheet.
    - Roast in the preheated oven for 20-25 minutes, or until vegetables are tender and lightly browned. Set aside.
2. **Prepare Ramen Noodles:**
    - In a large pot, bring water to a boil and cook the ramen noodles according to the package instructions. Drain and rinse under cold water to stop cooking. Divide the noodles among serving bowls.
3. **Make the Broth:**
    - In the same pot used for noodles (or a separate pot if needed), heat vegetable oil over medium heat. Add minced garlic and grated ginger, sauté for 1-2 minutes until fragrant.

- Add vegetable broth, soy sauce (or tamari), miso paste, sesame oil, rice vinegar, and maple syrup or agave syrup. Stir well to combine.
- Bring the broth to a simmer and let it cook for about 5 minutes to allow the flavors to meld together. Taste and adjust seasoning with soy sauce or salt if needed.

4. **Assemble the Ramen Bowls:**
   - Divide the cooked ramen noodles among serving bowls.
   - Ladle the hot broth over the noodles.
   - Add roasted vegetables, sliced mushrooms, baby spinach, and sliced bamboo shoots to each bowl.
5. **Garnish and Serve:**
   - Garnish each bowl with chopped green onions, nori strips, and sesame seeds.
6. **Enjoy!**
   - Serve hot and enjoy your flavorful Vegetarian Ramen with Roasted Vegetables!

This recipe serves 2-4 people depending on portion sizes. Adjust the ingredients accordingly for larger servings. It's a hearty and satisfying dish that celebrates the natural flavors of vegetables in a comforting ramen bowl.

Chicken Ramen with Nori and Scallions

Ingredients:

For the Chicken:

- 2 boneless, skinless chicken breasts
- Salt and pepper, to taste
- 1 tbsp vegetable oil

For the Ramen:

- 2 packs of ramen noodles (discard seasoning packets)
- 6 cups chicken broth
- 4 cloves garlic, minced
- 1-inch piece of ginger, grated
- 2 tbsp soy sauce
- 1 tbsp mirin (Japanese sweet rice wine)
- 1 tbsp sake (optional)
- 1 tbsp sesame oil
- 1 tbsp vegetable oil
- 2 green onions, chopped (white and green parts separated)
- 4 sheets of nori (seaweed), cut into strips
- Sesame seeds, for garnish

Instructions:

1. **Prepare the Chicken:**
    - Season chicken breasts with salt and pepper on both sides.
    - Heat vegetable oil in a skillet over medium-high heat. Add chicken breasts and cook for about 6-7 minutes per side, or until fully cooked and internal temperature reaches 165°F (74°C). Remove from skillet and let rest for a few minutes. Slice or shred the chicken into bite-sized pieces.
2. **Prepare Ramen Noodles:**
    - In a large pot, bring water to a boil and cook the ramen noodles according to the package instructions. Drain and rinse under cold water to stop cooking. Divide the noodles among serving bowls.
3. **Make the Broth:**
    - In the same pot used for noodles (or a separate pot if needed), heat vegetable oil over medium heat. Add minced garlic and grated ginger, sauté for 1-2 minutes until fragrant.
    - Pour in chicken broth, soy sauce, mirin, sake (if using), and sesame oil. Bring to a simmer and let it cook for about 5 minutes to allow the flavors to meld together. Taste and adjust seasoning with soy sauce or salt if needed.
4. **Assemble the Ramen Bowls:**

        - Divide the cooked ramen noodles among serving bowls.
        - Ladle the hot broth over the noodles.
        - Add sliced or shredded chicken pieces to each bowl.
5. **Garnish and Serve:**
        - Garnish each bowl with chopped green onions, nori strips, and sesame seeds.
6. **Enjoy!**
        - Serve hot and enjoy your delicious Chicken Ramen with Nori and Scallions!

This recipe serves 2-4 people depending on portion sizes. Adjust the ingredients accordingly for larger servings. It's a comforting and flavorful dish that's perfect for any time of the year.

Pork Ramen with Kimchi and Egg

Ingredients:

For the Pork:

- 1 lb pork belly or pork shoulder, thinly sliced
- Salt and pepper, to taste
- 1 tbsp vegetable oil

For the Ramen:

- 2 packs of ramen noodles (discard seasoning packets)
- 6 cups pork or chicken broth
- 1 cup kimchi, chopped
- 4 cloves garlic, minced
- 1-inch piece of ginger, grated
- 2 tbsp soy sauce
- 1 tbsp mirin (Japanese sweet rice wine)
- 1 tbsp sesame oil
- 1 tbsp vegetable oil
- 2 green onions, chopped (white and green parts separated)
- 4 eggs, soft-boiled
- Sesame seeds, for garnish

Instructions:

1. **Prepare the Pork:**
   - Season pork slices with salt and pepper.
   - Heat vegetable oil in a large skillet or pan over medium-high heat. Add pork slices and cook until browned and cooked through, about 3-4 minutes per side. Remove from skillet and set aside.
2. **Prepare Ramen Noodles:**
   - In a large pot, bring water to a boil and cook the ramen noodles according to the package instructions. Drain and rinse under cold water to stop cooking. Divide the noodles among serving bowls.
3. **Make the Broth:**
   - In the same pot used for noodles (or a separate pot if needed), heat vegetable oil over medium heat. Add minced garlic and grated ginger, sauté for 1-2 minutes until fragrant.
   - Pour in pork or chicken broth, soy sauce, mirin, and sesame oil. Bring to a simmer and let it cook for about 5 minutes to allow the flavors to meld together. Taste and adjust seasoning with soy sauce or salt if needed.
4. **Assemble the Ramen Bowls:**
   - Divide the cooked ramen noodles among serving bowls.

- Ladle the hot broth over the noodles.
- Add chopped kimchi to each bowl.

5. **Prepare the Soft-Boiled Eggs:**
    - Bring a separate pot of water to a boil. Carefully add the eggs and cook for 6-7 minutes for a soft-boiled egg (adjust timing for desired yolk consistency). Remove eggs with a slotted spoon and place them in cold water to stop cooking. Peel and halve the eggs.
6. **Finish and Serve:**
    - Divide the cooked pork slices among the ramen bowls.
    - Place a soft-boiled egg half on top of each bowl.
    - Garnish with chopped green onions and sesame seeds.
7. **Enjoy!**
    - Serve hot and enjoy your delicious Pork Ramen with Kimchi and Egg!

This recipe serves 4 people. Adjust the ingredients accordingly for larger or smaller servings. It's a hearty and satisfying ramen dish with a delightful blend of flavors from the pork, tangy kimchi, and creamy egg.

Beef Ramen with Ginger and Garlic

Ingredients:

For the Beef:

- 1 lb beef sirloin or flank steak, thinly sliced
- Salt and pepper, to taste
- 1 tbsp vegetable oil

For the Ramen:

- 2 packs of ramen noodles (discard seasoning packets)
- 6 cups beef broth
- 4 cloves garlic, minced
- 1-inch piece of ginger, grated
- 2 tbsp soy sauce
- 1 tbsp mirin (Japanese sweet rice wine)
- 1 tbsp sesame oil
- 1 tbsp vegetable oil
- 2 green onions, chopped (white and green parts separated)
- Optional: sliced mushrooms, baby spinach, bamboo shoots
- Sesame seeds, for garnish

Instructions:

1. **Prepare the Beef:**
   - Season beef slices with salt and pepper.
   - Heat vegetable oil in a large skillet or pan over medium-high heat. Add beef slices and cook until browned and cooked through, about 2-3 minutes per side. Remove from skillet and set aside.
2. **Prepare Ramen Noodles:**
   - In a large pot, bring water to a boil and cook the ramen noodles according to the package instructions. Drain and rinse under cold water to stop cooking. Divide the noodles among serving bowls.
3. **Make the Broth:**
   - In the same pot used for noodles (or a separate pot if needed), heat vegetable oil over medium heat. Add minced garlic and grated ginger, sauté for 1-2 minutes until fragrant.
   - Pour in beef broth, soy sauce, mirin, and sesame oil. Bring to a simmer and let it cook for about 5 minutes to allow the flavors to meld together. Taste and adjust seasoning with soy sauce or salt if needed.
4. **Assemble the Ramen Bowls:**
   - Divide the cooked ramen noodles among serving bowls.
   - Ladle the hot broth over the noodles.

- Add cooked beef slices to each bowl.
5. **Add Optional Ingredients:**
    - If desired, add sliced mushrooms, baby spinach, and bamboo shoots to each bowl.
6. **Garnish and Serve:**
    - Garnish each bowl with chopped green onions and sesame seeds.
7. **Enjoy!**
    - Serve hot and enjoy your delicious Beef Ramen with Ginger and Garlic!

This recipe serves 4 people. Adjust the ingredients accordingly for larger or smaller servings. It's a comforting and flavorful ramen dish that's perfect for any occasion.

Salmon Ramen with Wakame and Soy

Ingredients:

For the Salmon:

- 2 salmon fillets, skinless
- Salt and pepper, to taste
- 1 tbsp vegetable oil

For the Ramen:

- 2 packs of ramen noodles (discard seasoning packets)
- 6 cups fish or vegetable broth
- 1/4 cup soy sauce
- 1 tbsp mirin (Japanese sweet rice wine)
- 1 tbsp sesame oil
- 1 tbsp vegetable oil
- 4 cloves garlic, minced
- 1-inch piece of ginger, grated
- 2 tbsp dried wakame seaweed, rehydrated according to package instructions
- 2 green onions, chopped (white and green parts separated)
- 1 tbsp rice vinegar (optional)
- Sesame seeds, for garnish

Instructions:

1. **Prepare the Salmon:**
   - Season salmon fillets with salt and pepper on both sides.
   - Heat vegetable oil in a skillet over medium-high heat. Add salmon fillets, skin-side down, and cook for 4-5 minutes until crispy. Flip and cook for another 3-4 minutes until salmon is cooked through and flakes easily with a fork. Remove from skillet and set aside.
2. **Prepare Ramen Noodles:**
   - In a large pot, bring water to a boil and cook the ramen noodles according to the package instructions. Drain and rinse under cold water to stop cooking. Divide the noodles among serving bowls.
3. **Make the Broth:**
   - In the same pot used for noodles (or a separate pot if needed), heat vegetable oil over medium heat. Add minced garlic and grated ginger, sauté for 1-2 minutes until fragrant.
   - Pour in fish or vegetable broth, soy sauce, mirin, sesame oil, and rehydrated wakame seaweed. Bring to a simmer and let it cook for about 5 minutes to allow the flavors to meld together. Taste and adjust seasoning with soy sauce or salt if needed. Add rice vinegar if desired for a slight tang.

4. **Assemble the Ramen Bowls:**
    - Divide the cooked ramen noodles among serving bowls.
    - Ladle the hot broth over the noodles.
    - Flake the cooked salmon fillets and distribute evenly among the bowls.
5. **Garnish and Serve:**
    - Garnish each bowl with chopped green onions and sesame seeds.
6. **Enjoy!**
    - Serve hot and enjoy your delicious Salmon Ramen with Wakame and Soy!

This recipe serves 2-4 people depending on portion sizes. Adjust the ingredients accordingly for larger servings. It's a comforting and nutritious ramen dish with the delicate flavor of salmon and the umami richness of wakame and soy.

Lamb Ramen with Harissa

Ingredients:

For the Lamb:

- 1 lb lamb shoulder or leg, thinly sliced
- Salt and pepper, to taste
- 2 tbsp harissa paste
- 1 tbsp olive oil

For the Ramen:

- 2 packs of ramen noodles (discard seasoning packets)
- 6 cups beef or lamb broth
- 4 cloves garlic, minced
- 1-inch piece of ginger, grated
- 2 tbsp soy sauce
- 1 tbsp mirin (Japanese sweet rice wine)
- 1 tbsp sesame oil
- 1 tbsp vegetable oil
- 2 green onions, chopped (white and green parts separated)
- 1 tbsp rice vinegar (optional)
- Fresh cilantro, chopped, for garnish
- Sesame seeds, for garnish

Instructions:

1. **Prepare the Lamb:**
    - Season lamb slices with salt and pepper.
    - In a bowl, mix harissa paste and olive oil. Rub the harissa mixture all over the lamb slices, ensuring they are well coated. Let marinate for at least 30 minutes.
2. **Cook the Lamb:**
    - Heat a large skillet or pan over medium-high heat. Add the marinated lamb slices and cook for about 3-4 minutes per side, or until browned and cooked to your desired doneness. Remove from skillet and set aside.
3. **Prepare Ramen Noodles:**
    - In a large pot, bring water to a boil and cook the ramen noodles according to the package instructions. Drain and rinse under cold water to stop cooking. Divide the noodles among serving bowls.
4. **Make the Broth:**
    - In the same pot used for noodles (or a separate pot if needed), heat vegetable oil over medium heat. Add minced garlic and grated ginger, sauté for 1-2 minutes until fragrant.

- Pour in beef or lamb broth, soy sauce, mirin, sesame oil, and rice vinegar (if using). Bring to a simmer and let it cook for about 5 minutes to allow the flavors to meld together. Taste and adjust seasoning with soy sauce or salt if needed.
5. **Assemble the Ramen Bowls:**
    - Divide the cooked ramen noodles among serving bowls.
    - Ladle the hot broth over the noodles.
    - Arrange the cooked lamb slices on top of each bowl.
6. **Garnish and Serve:**
    - Garnish each bowl with chopped green onions, fresh cilantro, and sesame seeds.
7. **Enjoy!**
    - Serve hot and enjoy your flavorful Lamb Ramen with Harissa!

This recipe serves 2-4 people depending on portion sizes. Adjust the ingredients accordingly for larger servings. It's a unique and spicy twist on traditional ramen, perfect for those who enjoy bold and adventurous flavors.

Vegan Ramen with Spicy Miso Broth

Ingredients:

For the Spicy Miso Broth:

- 6 cups vegetable broth
- 4 cloves garlic, minced
- 1-inch piece of ginger, grated
- 2 tbsp miso paste (white or red)
- 2 tbsp soy sauce (or tamari for gluten-free option)
- 1 tbsp sesame oil
- 1 tbsp vegetable oil
- 1 tbsp sriracha sauce (adjust to taste for spiciness)
- 1 tbsp rice vinegar
- 1 tbsp maple syrup or agave syrup
- Salt and pepper, to taste

For the Ramen:

- 2 packs of ramen noodles (discard seasoning packets)
- 1 block firm tofu, cut into cubes
- 2 cups sliced shiitake mushrooms
- 2 cups baby spinach or bok choy
- 2 green onions, chopped (white and green parts separated)
- Sesame seeds, for garnish
- Nori (seaweed), sliced into strips, for garnish (optional)

Instructions:

1. **Prepare the Spicy Miso Broth:**
   - In a large pot, heat vegetable oil over medium heat. Add minced garlic and grated ginger, sauté for 1-2 minutes until fragrant.
   - Add vegetable broth, miso paste, soy sauce, sesame oil, sriracha sauce, rice vinegar, and maple syrup or agave syrup. Stir well to combine.
   - Bring the broth to a simmer and let it cook for about 10-15 minutes, stirring occasionally. Taste and adjust seasoning with salt and pepper if needed. Keep warm on low heat while preparing the rest.
2. **Prepare Ramen Noodles:**
   - In a separate pot, bring water to a boil and cook the ramen noodles according to the package instructions. Drain and rinse under cold water to stop cooking. Divide the noodles among serving bowls.
3. **Prepare Tofu and Mushrooms:**
   - In a non-stick skillet, heat a small amount of vegetable oil over medium-high heat. Add tofu cubes and cook until golden brown on all sides. Remove from skillet and set aside.

- In the same skillet, add sliced shiitake mushrooms and sauté until tender, about 5-7 minutes. Set aside.

4. **Assemble the Ramen Bowls:**
   - Divide the cooked ramen noodles among serving bowls.
   - Pour the hot spicy miso broth over the noodles.
   - Add sautéed mushrooms, tofu cubes, and baby spinach or bok choy to each bowl.

5. **Garnish and Serve:**
   - Garnish each bowl with chopped green onions, sesame seeds, and nori strips (if using).

6. **Enjoy!**
   - Serve hot and enjoy your delicious Vegan Ramen with Spicy Miso Broth!

This recipe serves 2-4 people depending on portion sizes. Adjust the ingredients accordingly for larger servings. It's a hearty and flavorful vegan ramen dish that will warm you up and satisfy your taste buds with its spicy and savory broth.

Chicken Ramen with Shiitake and Mirin

Ingredients:

For the Chicken:

- 2 boneless, skinless chicken breasts
- Salt and pepper, to taste
- 1 tbsp vegetable oil

For the Ramen:

- 2 packs of ramen noodles (discard seasoning packets)
- 6 cups chicken broth
- 1 cup sliced shiitake mushrooms
- 4 cloves garlic, minced
- 1-inch piece of ginger, grated
- 2 tbsp soy sauce
- 2 tbsp mirin (Japanese sweet rice wine)
- 1 tbsp sesame oil
- 1 tbsp vegetable oil
- 2 green onions, chopped (white and green parts separated)
- 1 tbsp rice vinegar (optional)
- Sesame seeds, for garnish

Instructions:

1. **Prepare the Chicken:**
    - Season chicken breasts with salt and pepper on both sides.
    - Heat vegetable oil in a large skillet or pan over medium-high heat. Add chicken breasts and cook for about 6-7 minutes per side, or until fully cooked and internal temperature reaches 165°F (74°C). Remove from skillet and let rest for a few minutes. Slice or shred the chicken into bite-sized pieces.
2. **Prepare Ramen Noodles:**
    - In a large pot, bring water to a boil and cook the ramen noodles according to the package instructions. Drain and rinse under cold water to stop cooking. Divide the noodles among serving bowls.
3. **Make the Broth:**
    - In the same pot used for noodles (or a separate pot if needed), heat vegetable oil over medium heat. Add minced garlic and grated ginger, sauté for 1-2 minutes until fragrant.
    - Pour in chicken broth, soy sauce, mirin, and sesame oil. Bring to a simmer and let it cook for about 5 minutes to allow the flavors to meld together. Taste and adjust seasoning with soy sauce or salt if needed. Add rice vinegar if desired for a slight tang.
4. **Add Shiitake Mushrooms:**

- Add sliced shiitake mushrooms to the broth and simmer for an additional 3-4 minutes until mushrooms are tender.
5. **Assemble the Ramen Bowls:**
    - Divide the cooked ramen noodles among serving bowls.
    - Ladle the hot broth and shiitake mushrooms over the noodles.
    - Add sliced or shredded chicken pieces to each bowl.
6. **Garnish and Serve:**
    - Garnish each bowl with chopped green onions and sesame seeds.
7. **Enjoy!**
    - Serve hot and enjoy your delicious Chicken Ramen with Shiitake and Mirin!

This recipe serves 2-4 people depending on portion sizes. Adjust the ingredients accordingly for larger servings. It's a comforting and flavorful ramen dish that combines the earthy flavor of shiitake mushrooms with the sweetness of mirin, perfect for any occasion.

Pork Ramen with Black Garlic Oil

Ingredients:

For the Pork:

- 1 lb pork belly or pork shoulder, thinly sliced
- Salt and pepper, to taste
- 1 tbsp vegetable oil

For the Black Garlic Oil:

- 1/2 cup vegetable oil
- 4 cloves black garlic, minced
- 1 tbsp soy sauce
- 1 tbsp mirin (Japanese sweet rice wine)

For the Ramen:

- 2 packs of ramen noodles (discard seasoning packets)
- 6 cups pork or chicken broth
- 4 cloves garlic, minced
- 1-inch piece of ginger, grated
- 2 tbsp soy sauce
- 1 tbsp mirin
- 1 tbsp sesame oil
- 1 tbsp vegetable oil
- 2 green onions, chopped (white and green parts separated)
- Optional: sliced bamboo shoots, nori (seaweed), soft-boiled egg
- Sesame seeds, for garnish

Instructions:

Prepare the Pork:

1. Season pork slices with salt and pepper.
2. Heat vegetable oil in a large skillet or pan over medium-high heat. Add pork slices and cook until browned and cooked through, about 3-4 minutes per side. Remove from skillet and set aside.

Prepare the Black Garlic Oil:

1. In a small saucepan, heat vegetable oil over medium-low heat.
2. Add minced black garlic and cook gently for 3-4 minutes until fragrant and softened.
3. Remove from heat and stir in soy sauce and mirin. Set aside.

Prepare Ramen Noodles:

1. In a large pot, bring water to a boil and cook the ramen noodles according to the package instructions. Drain and rinse under cold water to stop cooking. Divide the noodles among serving bowls.

Make the Broth:

1. In the same pot used for noodles (or a separate pot if needed), heat vegetable oil over medium heat. Add minced garlic and grated ginger, sauté for 1-2 minutes until fragrant.
2. Pour in pork or chicken broth, soy sauce, mirin, and sesame oil. Bring to a simmer and let it cook for about 5 minutes to allow the flavors to meld together. Taste and adjust seasoning with soy sauce or salt if needed.

Assemble the Ramen Bowls:

1. Divide the cooked ramen noodles among serving bowls.
2. Ladle the hot broth over the noodles.
3. Add cooked pork slices to each bowl.

Finish and Serve:

1. Drizzle each bowl with black garlic oil.
2. Garnish with chopped green onions, and sesame seeds.
3. Add optional toppings like sliced bamboo shoots, nori, or soft-boiled egg if desired.

Enjoy! Serve hot and enjoy your delicious Pork Ramen with Black Garlic Oil! Adjust the ingredients and seasonings to your taste preferences. This recipe serves 2-4 people depending on portion sizes. It's a comforting and flavorful ramen dish that showcases the unique umami of black garlic oil.

Beef Ramen with Sichuan Peppercorns

Ingredients:

For the Beef:

- 1 lb beef sirloin or flank steak, thinly sliced
- Salt and pepper, to taste
- 1 tbsp vegetable oil

For the Ramen:

- 2 packs of ramen noodles (discard seasoning packets)
- 6 cups beef broth
- 4 cloves garlic, minced
- 1-inch piece of ginger, grated
- 2 tbsp soy sauce
- 1 tbsp mirin (Japanese sweet rice wine)
- 1 tbsp sesame oil
- 1 tbsp vegetable oil
- 1 tbsp Sichuan peppercorns
- 2 green onions, chopped (white and green parts separated)
- Optional: sliced bamboo shoots, baby bok choy
- Sesame seeds, for garnish

Instructions:

1. **Prepare the Beef:**
   - Season beef slices with salt and pepper.
   - Heat vegetable oil in a large skillet or pan over medium-high heat. Add beef slices and cook until browned and cooked through, about 2-3 minutes per side. Remove from skillet and set aside.
2. **Prepare Ramen Noodles:**
   - In a large pot, bring water to a boil and cook the ramen noodles according to the package instructions. Drain and rinse under cold water to stop cooking. Divide the noodles among serving bowls.
3. **Make the Broth:**
   - In the same pot used for noodles (or a separate pot if needed), heat vegetable oil over medium heat. Add minced garlic, grated ginger, and Sichuan peppercorns. Sauté for 1-2 minutes until fragrant.
   - Pour in beef broth, soy sauce, mirin, and sesame oil. Bring to a simmer and let it cook for about 5 minutes to allow the flavors to meld together. Taste and adjust seasoning with soy sauce or salt if needed.
4. **Assemble the Ramen Bowls:**
   - Divide the cooked ramen noodles among serving bowls.
   - Ladle the hot broth over the noodles.
   - Add cooked beef slices to each bowl.

5. **Add Optional Ingredients:**
   - If desired, add sliced bamboo shoots and baby bok choy to each bowl.
6. **Garnish and Serve:**
   - Garnish each bowl with chopped green onions and sesame seeds.
7. **Enjoy!**
   - Serve hot and enjoy your delicious Beef Ramen with Sichuan Peppercorns!

This recipe serves 2-4 people depending on portion sizes. Adjust the ingredients accordingly for larger servings. It's a flavorful and aromatic ramen dish with a delightful numbing sensation from the Sichuan peppercorns, perfect for those who enjoy bold and spicy flavors.

Shrimp Ramen with Lemongrass and Coconut Milk

Ingredients:

For the Shrimp:

- 1 lb shrimp, peeled and deveined
- Salt and pepper, to taste
- 1 tbsp vegetable oil

For the Ramen:

- 2 packs of ramen noodles (discard seasoning packets)
- 6 cups chicken or vegetable broth
- 1 can (13.5 oz) coconut milk
- 2 stalks lemongrass, bruised and chopped into segments
- 4 cloves garlic, minced
- 1-inch piece of ginger, grated
- 2 tbsp soy sauce (or tamari for gluten-free option)
- 1 tbsp fish sauce (optional, for additional depth of flavor)
- 1 tbsp vegetable oil
- 1 tbsp lime juice
- 1 tbsp brown sugar or honey
- 1 red chili, sliced (optional for spice)
- Fresh cilantro, chopped, for garnish
- Lime wedges, for serving

Instructions:

1. **Prepare the Shrimp:**
    - Season shrimp with salt and pepper.
    - Heat vegetable oil in a large skillet or pan over medium-high heat. Add shrimp and cook for about 2-3 minutes per side until pink and cooked through. Remove from skillet and set aside.
2. **Prepare Ramen Noodles:**
    - In a large pot, bring water to a boil and cook the ramen noodles according to the package instructions. Drain and rinse under cold water to stop cooking. Divide the noodles among serving bowls.
3. **Make the Lemongrass Coconut Broth:**
    - In the same pot used for noodles (or a separate pot if needed), heat vegetable oil over medium heat. Add minced garlic, grated ginger, and chopped lemongrass segments. Sauté for 1-2 minutes until fragrant.
    - Pour in chicken or vegetable broth, coconut milk, soy sauce, fish sauce (if using), lime juice, and brown sugar or honey. Bring to a simmer and let it cook for about 10-15 minutes to infuse the flavors. Taste and adjust seasoning with soy sauce or salt if needed. Remove the lemongrass segments before serving.
4. **Assemble the Ramen Bowls:**

- Divide the cooked ramen noodles among serving bowls.
- Ladle the hot lemongrass coconut broth over the noodles.
- Arrange cooked shrimp on top of each bowl.
5. **Garnish and Serve:**
    - Garnish each bowl with sliced red chili (if using), chopped fresh cilantro, and lime wedges on the side.
6. **Enjoy!**
    - Serve hot and enjoy your delicious Shrimp Ramen with Lemongrass and Coconut Milk!

This recipe serves 2-4 people depending on portion sizes. Adjust the ingredients accordingly for larger servings. It's a refreshing and aromatic ramen dish that combines the delicate sweetness of coconut milk with the citrusy notes of lemongrass, perfect for a light yet satisfying meal.

Vegan Ramen with Crispy Tofu

Ingredients:

For the Crispy Tofu:

- 1 block firm tofu, drained and pressed
- 2 tbsp cornstarch
- 1 tbsp soy sauce
- 1 tbsp sesame oil
- 1 tbsp vegetable oil

For the Ramen:

- 2 packs of ramen noodles (discard seasoning packets)
- 6 cups vegetable broth
- 4 cloves garlic, minced
- 1-inch piece of ginger, grated
- 2 tbsp soy sauce (or tamari for gluten-free option)
- 1 tbsp miso paste
- 1 tbsp sesame oil
- 1 tbsp vegetable oil
- 1 cup sliced shiitake mushrooms
- 2 cups baby spinach or bok choy
- 2 green onions, chopped (white and green parts separated)
- Optional: sliced bamboo shoots, nori (seaweed), sesame seeds
- Chili oil or sriracha, for serving (optional)

Instructions:

Prepare the Crispy Tofu:

1. Cut the tofu into cubes or rectangles.
2. In a bowl, toss the tofu cubes with cornstarch until evenly coated.
3. Heat vegetable oil in a non-stick skillet over medium-high heat. Add tofu cubes in a single layer and cook until crispy and golden brown on all sides, about 4-5 minutes per side. Remove from skillet and set aside.

Prepare Ramen Noodles:

1. In a large pot, bring water to a boil and cook the ramen noodles according to the package instructions. Drain and rinse under cold water to stop cooking. Divide the noodles among serving bowls.

Make the Ramen Broth:

1. In the same pot used for noodles (or a separate pot if needed), heat vegetable oil over medium heat. Add minced garlic and grated ginger, sauté for 1-2 minutes until fragrant.

2. Pour in vegetable broth, soy sauce, miso paste, and sesame oil. Bring to a simmer and let it cook for about 5 minutes to allow the flavors to meld together. Taste and adjust seasoning with soy sauce or salt if needed.

Assemble the Ramen Bowls:

1. Divide the cooked ramen noodles among serving bowls.
2. Ladle the hot broth over the noodles.
3. Add sliced shiitake mushrooms and baby spinach or bok choy to each bowl.

Garnish and Serve:

1. Top each bowl with crispy tofu cubes and chopped green onions.
2. Add optional toppings like sliced bamboo shoots, nori, sesame seeds, and a drizzle of chili oil or sriracha for extra spice if desired.

Enjoy! Serve hot and enjoy your delicious Vegan Ramen with Crispy Tofu! This recipe serves 2-4 people depending on portion sizes. Adjust the ingredients accordingly for larger servings. It's a satisfying and flavorful vegan ramen dish that showcases crispy tofu and a savory broth packed with umami flavors.

Duck Ramen with Hoisin Sauce

Ingredients:

For the Duck:

- 2 duck breasts
- Salt and pepper, to taste
- 1 tbsp vegetable oil

For the Ramen:

- 2 packs of ramen noodles (discard seasoning packets)
- 6 cups chicken or duck broth
- 4 cloves garlic, minced
- 1-inch piece of ginger, grated
- 2 tbsp soy sauce
- 2 tbsp hoisin sauce
- 1 tbsp rice vinegar
- 1 tbsp sesame oil
- 1 tbsp vegetable oil
- 1 cup sliced shiitake mushrooms
- 2 cups baby spinach or bok choy
- 2 green onions, chopped (white and green parts separated)
- Optional: sliced bamboo shoots, nori (seaweed), sesame seeds

Instructions:

Prepare the Duck:

1. Score the skin of the duck breasts in a crosshatch pattern. This helps the fat render and crisps up the skin.
2. Season the duck breasts with salt and pepper on both sides.
3. Heat vegetable oil in a skillet over medium-high heat. Place the duck breasts in the skillet, skin side down, and cook for about 5-6 minutes until the skin is crispy and golden brown. Flip and cook for another 3-4 minutes for medium-rare or longer to your desired doneness. Remove from heat and let the duck rest for a few minutes before slicing thinly.

Prepare Ramen Noodles:

1. In a large pot, bring water to a boil and cook the ramen noodles according to the package instructions. Drain and rinse under cold water to stop cooking. Divide the noodles among serving bowls.

Make the Ramen Broth:

1. In the same pot used for noodles (or a separate pot if needed), heat vegetable oil over medium heat. Add minced garlic and grated ginger, sauté for 1-2 minutes until fragrant.

2. Pour in chicken or duck broth, soy sauce, hoisin sauce, rice vinegar, and sesame oil. Bring to a simmer and let it cook for about 5 minutes to allow the flavors to meld together. Taste and adjust seasoning with soy sauce or salt if needed.

Assemble the Ramen Bowls:

1. Divide the cooked ramen noodles among serving bowls.
2. Ladle the hot broth over the noodles.
3. Add sliced shiitake mushrooms and baby spinach or bok choy to each bowl.

Garnish and Serve:

1. Arrange slices of cooked duck breast on top of each bowl.
2. Garnish with chopped green onions and any optional toppings like sliced bamboo shoots, nori, or sesame seeds.

Enjoy! Serve hot and enjoy your delicious Duck Ramen with Hoisin Sauce! This recipe serves 2-4 people depending on portion sizes. Adjust the ingredients accordingly for larger servings. It's a decadent and savory ramen dish that highlights the rich flavors of duck and the sweet-savory notes of hoisin sauce.

Beef Ramen with Ponzu and Mirin

Ingredients:

For the Beef:

- 1 lb beef sirloin or flank steak, thinly sliced
- Salt and pepper, to taste
- 1 tbsp vegetable oil

For the Ramen:

- 2 packs of ramen noodles (discard seasoning packets)
- 6 cups beef broth
- 1/4 cup ponzu sauce
- 2 tbsp mirin (Japanese sweet rice wine)
- 2 cloves garlic, minced
- 1-inch piece of ginger, grated
- 1 tbsp soy sauce
- 1 tbsp sesame oil
- 1 tbsp vegetable oil
- 2 green onions, chopped (white and green parts separated)
- Optional: sliced bamboo shoots, nori (seaweed), sesame seeds
- Lime wedges, for serving

Instructions:

Prepare the Beef:

1. Season beef slices with salt and pepper.
2. Heat vegetable oil in a large skillet or pan over medium-high heat. Add beef slices and cook until browned and cooked through, about 2-3 minutes per side. Remove from skillet and set aside.

Prepare Ramen Noodles:

1. In a large pot, bring water to a boil and cook the ramen noodles according to the package instructions. Drain and rinse under cold water to stop cooking. Divide the noodles among serving bowls.

Make the Ramen Broth:

1. In the same pot used for noodles (or a separate pot if needed), heat vegetable oil over medium heat. Add minced garlic and grated ginger, sauté for 1-2 minutes until fragrant.
2. Pour in beef broth, ponzu sauce, mirin, soy sauce, and sesame oil. Bring to a simmer and let it cook for about 5 minutes to allow the flavors to meld together. Taste and adjust seasoning with soy sauce or salt if needed.

Assemble the Ramen Bowls:

1. Divide the cooked ramen noodles among serving bowls.
2. Ladle the hot broth over the noodles.
3. Add cooked beef slices to each bowl.

Garnish and Serve:

1. Garnish each bowl with chopped green onions, and optional toppings like sliced bamboo shoots, nori, and sesame seeds.
2. Serve with lime wedges on the side for squeezing over the ramen.

Enjoy! Serve hot and enjoy your delicious Beef Ramen with Ponzu and Mirin! This recipe serves 2-4 people depending on portion sizes. Adjust the ingredients accordingly for larger servings. It's a delightful fusion of flavors that brings out the umami of beef with the citrusy tang of ponzu and the sweetness of mirin.

Chicken Ramen with Soy-Marinated Egg

Ingredients:

For the Chicken:

- 2 boneless, skinless chicken breasts
- Salt and pepper, to taste
- 1 tbsp vegetable oil

For the Soy-Marinated Eggs (Ajitsuke Tamago):

- 4 large eggs
- 1/2 cup soy sauce
- 1/4 cup mirin (Japanese sweet rice wine)
- 1/4 cup water
- 2 tbsp sugar

For the Ramen:

- 2 packs of ramen noodles (discard seasoning packets)
- 6 cups chicken broth
- 4 cloves garlic, minced
- 1-inch piece of ginger, grated
- 2 tbsp soy sauce
- 1 tbsp sesame oil
- 1 tbsp vegetable oil
- 2 green onions, chopped (white and green parts separated)
- Optional: sliced bamboo shoots, nori (seaweed), sesame seeds, chili oil

Instructions:

Prepare the Soy-Marinated Eggs (Ajitsuke Tamago):

1. In a saucepan, bring water to a boil. Gently add the eggs and boil for 6-7 minutes for a slightly soft center. Remove the eggs and immediately transfer to an ice bath to cool.
2. In a bowl, mix together soy sauce, mirin, water, and sugar until the sugar dissolves.
3. Peel the cooled eggs and place them in the soy sauce mixture, ensuring they are fully submerged. Marinate in the refrigerator for at least 2 hours, preferably overnight, turning occasionally to ensure even marination.

Prepare the Chicken:

1. Season chicken breasts with salt and pepper on both sides.
2. Heat vegetable oil in a large skillet or pan over medium-high heat. Add chicken breasts and cook for about 6-7 minutes per side, or until fully cooked and internal temperature reaches 165°F (74°C). Remove from skillet, let rest for a few minutes, then slice or shred into bite-sized pieces.

Prepare Ramen Noodles:

1. In a large pot, bring water to a boil and cook the ramen noodles according to the package instructions. Drain and rinse under cold water to stop cooking. Divide the noodles among serving bowls.

Make the Ramen Broth:

1. In the same pot used for noodles (or a separate pot if needed), heat vegetable oil over medium heat. Add minced garlic and grated ginger, sauté for 1-2 minutes until fragrant.
2. Pour in chicken broth, soy sauce, and sesame oil. Bring to a simmer and let it cook for about 5 minutes to allow the flavors to meld together. Taste and adjust seasoning with soy sauce or salt if needed.

Assemble the Ramen Bowls:

1. Divide the cooked ramen noodles among serving bowls.
2. Ladle the hot broth over the noodles.
3. Add cooked chicken pieces to each bowl.

Prepare the Soy-Marinated Eggs (Ajitsuke Tamago):

1. Remove the marinated eggs from the soy sauce mixture and slice in half lengthwise. Place one or two halves on top of each bowl of ramen.

Garnish and Serve:

1. Garnish each bowl with chopped green onions, and optional toppings like sliced bamboo shoots, nori, sesame seeds, and a drizzle of chili oil for extra spice if desired.

Enjoy! Serve hot and enjoy your delicious Chicken Ramen with Soy-Marinated Egg! This recipe serves 2-4 people depending on portion sizes. Adjust the ingredients accordingly for larger servings. It's a hearty and flavorful ramen dish that combines tender chicken with the umami-rich flavor of soy-marinated eggs.

Pork Ramen with Spicy Bean Paste

Ingredients:

For the Pork:

- 1 lb pork shoulder or pork belly, thinly sliced
- Salt and pepper, to taste
- 1 tbsp vegetable oil

For the Ramen:

- 2 packs of ramen noodles (discard seasoning packets)
- 6 cups pork or chicken broth
- 2-3 tbsp spicy bean paste (such as doubanjiang or gochujang)
- 4 cloves garlic, minced
- 1-inch piece of ginger, grated
- 2 tbsp soy sauce
- 1 tbsp sesame oil
- 1 tbsp vegetable oil
- 2 green onions, chopped (white and green parts separated)
- Optional: sliced bamboo shoots, baby bok choy, soft-boiled eggs
- Sesame seeds, for garnish

Instructions:

Prepare the Pork:

1. Season pork slices with salt and pepper.
2. Heat vegetable oil in a large skillet or pan over medium-high heat. Add pork slices and cook until browned and cooked through, about 2-3 minutes per side. Remove from skillet and set aside.

Prepare Ramen Noodles:

1. In a large pot, bring water to a boil and cook the ramen noodles according to the package instructions. Drain and rinse under cold water to stop cooking. Divide the noodles among serving bowls.

Make the Ramen Broth:

1. In the same pot used for noodles (or a separate pot if needed), heat vegetable oil over medium heat. Add minced garlic and grated ginger, sauté for 1-2 minutes until fragrant.
2. Add spicy bean paste (doubanjiang or gochujang) and stir fry for another minute until fragrant.
3. Pour in pork or chicken broth, soy sauce, and sesame oil. Bring to a simmer and let it cook for about 5 minutes to allow the flavors to meld together. Taste and adjust seasoning with soy sauce or salt if needed.

Assemble the Ramen Bowls:

1. Divide the cooked ramen noodles among serving bowls.

2. Ladle the hot broth over the noodles.
3. Add cooked pork slices to each bowl.

Garnish and Serve:

1. Garnish each bowl with chopped green onions and sesame seeds.
2. Add optional toppings like sliced bamboo shoots, baby bok choy, or soft-boiled eggs if desired.

Enjoy! Serve hot and enjoy your delicious Pork Ramen with Spicy Bean Paste! This recipe serves 2-4 people depending on portion sizes. Adjust the ingredients accordingly for larger servings. It's a flavorful and satisfying ramen dish that combines the savory richness of pork with the spicy kick of bean paste.

Turkey Ramen with Sage Butter

Ingredients:

For the Turkey:

- 1 lb turkey breast or thigh meat, thinly sliced

- Salt and pepper, to taste
- 1 tbsp vegetable oil

For the Ramen:

- 2 packs of ramen noodles (discard seasoning packets)
- 6 cups chicken or turkey broth
- 4 cloves garlic, minced
- 1-inch piece of ginger, grated
- 2 tbsp soy sauce
- 1 tbsp sesame oil
- 1 tbsp vegetable oil
- 2 tbsp unsalted butter
- 10-12 fresh sage leaves
- 2 green onions, chopped (white and green parts separated)
- Optional: sliced bamboo shoots, baby spinach, soft-boiled egg
- Sesame seeds, for garnish

Instructions:

Prepare the Turkey:

1. Season turkey slices with salt and pepper.
2. Heat vegetable oil in a large skillet or pan over medium-high heat. Add turkey slices and cook until browned and cooked through, about 3-4 minutes per side. Remove from skillet and set aside.

Prepare Ramen Noodles:

1. In a large pot, bring water to a boil and cook the ramen noodles according to the package instructions. Drain and rinse under cold water to stop cooking. Divide the noodles among serving bowls.

Make the Sage Butter:

1. In the same skillet used for turkey (or a separate skillet if preferred), melt unsalted butter over medium heat.
2. Add fresh sage leaves and cook for 1-2 minutes until crisp and fragrant. Remove the sage leaves and set aside.

Make the Ramen Broth:

1. In the same pot used for noodles (or a separate pot if needed), heat vegetable oil over medium heat. Add minced garlic and grated ginger, sauté for 1-2 minutes until fragrant.

2. Pour in chicken or turkey broth, soy sauce, and sesame oil. Bring to a simmer and let it cook for about 5 minutes to allow the flavors to meld together. Taste and adjust seasoning with soy sauce or salt if needed.

Assemble the Ramen Bowls:

1. Divide the cooked ramen noodles among serving bowls.
2. Ladle the hot broth over the noodles.
3. Add cooked turkey slices to each bowl.

Garnish and Serve:

1. Drizzle each bowl with sage butter.
2. Garnish with chopped green onions, crispy sage leaves, and optional toppings like sliced bamboo shoots, baby spinach, or soft-boiled egg.
3. Sprinkle with sesame seeds for added texture and flavor.

Enjoy! Serve hot and enjoy your delicious Turkey Ramen with Sage Butter! This recipe serves 2-4 people depending on portion sizes. Adjust the ingredients accordingly for larger servings. It's a comforting and flavorful ramen dish that highlights the tender turkey with the aromatic richness of sage butter.

Seafood Ramen with Thai Curry Broth

Ingredients:

For the Seafood:

- 1/2 lb shrimp, peeled and deveined
- 1/2 lb squid, cleaned and sliced into rings
- 1/2 lb mussels or clams, cleaned and scrubbed
- Salt and pepper, to taste
- 1 tbsp vegetable oil

For the Ramen:

- 2 packs of ramen noodles (discard seasoning packets)
- 6 cups seafood or chicken broth
- 1 can (14 oz) coconut milk
- 2 tbsp Thai red curry paste
- 4 cloves garlic, minced
- 1-inch piece of ginger, grated
- 2 tbsp soy sauce
- 1 tbsp fish sauce
- 1 tbsp brown sugar
- 1 tbsp lime juice
- 1 tbsp vegetable oil
- 2 green onions, chopped (white and green parts separated)
- Optional: sliced bamboo shoots, baby bok choy, Thai basil leaves, cilantro leaves, lime wedges

Instructions:

Prepare the Seafood:

1. Season shrimp, squid, and mussels or clams with salt and pepper.
2. Heat vegetable oil in a large skillet or pan over medium-high heat. Add seafood and cook until shrimp turns pink, squid is opaque, and mussels or clams have opened (discard any that do not open). Remove seafood from skillet and set aside.

Prepare Ramen Noodles:

1. In a large pot, bring water to a boil and cook the ramen noodles according to the package instructions. Drain and rinse under cold water to stop cooking. Divide the noodles among serving bowls.

Make the Thai Curry Broth:

1. In the same pot used for noodles (or a separate pot if needed), heat vegetable oil over medium heat. Add minced garlic and grated ginger, sauté for 1-2 minutes until fragrant.
2. Stir in Thai red curry paste and cook for another minute.

3. Pour in seafood or chicken broth, coconut milk, soy sauce, fish sauce, brown sugar, and lime juice. Bring to a simmer and let it cook for about 5 minutes to allow the flavors to meld together. Taste and adjust seasoning with soy sauce, fish sauce, or lime juice if needed.

Assemble the Ramen Bowls:

1. Divide the cooked ramen noodles among serving bowls.
2. Ladle the hot Thai curry broth over the noodles.
3. Add cooked seafood to each bowl.

Garnish and Serve:

1. Garnish each bowl with chopped green onions, Thai basil leaves, cilantro leaves, and optional toppings like sliced bamboo shoots and baby bok choy.
2. Serve with lime wedges on the side for squeezing over the ramen.

Enjoy! Serve hot and enjoy your delicious Seafood Ramen with Thai Curry Broth! This recipe serves 2-4 people depending on portion sizes. Adjust the ingredients accordingly for larger servings. It's a flavorful and aromatic ramen dish that combines the richness of coconut milk with the bold flavors of Thai red curry and the freshness of seafood.

Vegan Ramen with Kimchi and Sesame

Ingredients:

For the Ramen:

- 2 packs of ramen noodles (discard seasoning packets)
- 6 cups vegetable broth
- 1 cup kimchi, chopped
- 4 cloves garlic, minced
- 1-inch piece of ginger, grated
- 2 tbsp soy sauce (or tamari for gluten-free option)
- 1 tbsp sesame oil
- 1 tbsp vegetable oil
- 2 green onions, chopped (white and green parts separated)
- Optional: sliced bamboo shoots, baby spinach, nori (seaweed), sesame seeds

Instructions:

Prepare Ramen Noodles:

1. In a large pot, bring water to a boil and cook the ramen noodles according to the package instructions. Drain and rinse under cold water to stop cooking. Divide the noodles among serving bowls.

Make the Ramen Broth:

1. In the same pot used for noodles (or a separate pot if needed), heat vegetable oil over medium heat. Add minced garlic and grated ginger, sauté for 1-2 minutes until fragrant.
2. Pour in vegetable broth and bring to a simmer.
3. Add chopped kimchi, soy sauce (or tamari), and sesame oil to the broth. Simmer for about 5 minutes to allow the flavors to meld together. Taste and adjust seasoning with soy sauce or salt if needed.

Assemble the Ramen Bowls:

1. Divide the cooked ramen noodles among serving bowls.
2. Ladle the hot kimchi broth over the noodles.

Garnish and Serve:

1. Garnish each bowl with chopped green onions and optional toppings like sliced bamboo shoots, baby spinach, nori, and sesame seeds.

Enjoy! Serve hot and enjoy your delicious Vegan Ramen with Kimchi and Sesame! This recipe serves 2-4 people depending on portion sizes. Adjust the ingredients accordingly for larger servings. It's a flavorful and satisfying vegan ramen dish that combines the spicy tanginess of kimchi with the nutty aroma of sesame oil, perfect for a comforting meal.

Beef Ramen with Mushrooms and Soy

Ingredients:

For the Beef:

- 1 lb beef sirloin or flank steak, thinly sliced
- Salt and pepper, to taste
- 1 tbsp vegetable oil

For the Ramen:

- 2 packs of ramen noodles (discard seasoning packets)
- 6 cups beef broth
- 1 cup sliced mushrooms (shiitake, cremini, or your choice)
- 4 cloves garlic, minced
- 1-inch piece of ginger, grated
- 2 tbsp soy sauce
- 1 tbsp sesame oil
- 1 tbsp vegetable oil
- 2 green onions, chopped (white and green parts separated)
- Optional: sliced bamboo shoots, baby spinach, nori (seaweed), sesame seeds

Instructions:

Prepare the Beef:

1. Season beef slices with salt and pepper.
2. Heat vegetable oil in a large skillet or pan over medium-high heat. Add beef slices and cook until browned and cooked through, about 2-3 minutes per side. Remove from skillet and set aside.

Prepare Ramen Noodles:

1. In a large pot, bring water to a boil and cook the ramen noodles according to the package instructions. Drain and rinse under cold water to stop cooking. Divide the noodles among serving bowls.

Make the Ramen Broth:

1. In the same pot used for noodles (or a separate pot if needed), heat vegetable oil over medium heat. Add minced garlic and grated ginger, sauté for 1-2 minutes until fragrant.
2. Add sliced mushrooms and cook for another 2-3 minutes until softened.
3. Pour in beef broth, soy sauce, and sesame oil. Bring to a simmer and let it cook for about 5 minutes to allow the flavors to meld together. Taste and adjust seasoning with soy sauce or salt if needed.

Assemble the Ramen Bowls:

1. Divide the cooked ramen noodles among serving bowls.

2. Ladle the hot broth over the noodles.
3. Add cooked beef slices to each bowl.

Garnish and Serve:

1. Garnish each bowl with chopped green onions and optional toppings like sliced bamboo shoots, baby spinach, nori, and sesame seeds.

Enjoy! Serve hot and enjoy your delicious Beef Ramen with Mushrooms and Soy! This recipe serves 2-4 people depending on portion sizes. Adjust the ingredients accordingly for larger servings. It's a hearty and flavorful ramen dish that combines tender beef with earthy mushrooms and the umami richness of soy sauce, perfect for a comforting meal.

Chicken Ramen with Charred Corn

Ingredients:

For the Chicken:

- 2 boneless, skinless chicken breasts
- Salt and pepper, to taste
- 1 tbsp vegetable oil

For the Ramen:

- 2 packs of ramen noodles (discard seasoning packets)
- 6 cups chicken broth
- Kernels from 2 ears of corn
- 4 cloves garlic, minced
- 1-inch piece of ginger, grated
- 2 tbsp soy sauce
- 1 tbsp sesame oil
- 1 tbsp vegetable oil
- 2 green onions, chopped (white and green parts separated)
- Optional: sliced bamboo shoots, baby bok choy, soft-boiled eggs
- Sesame seeds, for garnish

Instructions:

Prepare the Chicken:

1. Season chicken breasts with salt and pepper on both sides.
2. Heat vegetable oil in a large skillet or pan over medium-high heat. Add chicken breasts and cook for about 6-7 minutes per side, or until fully cooked and internal temperature reaches 165°F (74°C). Remove from skillet, let rest for a few minutes, then slice or shred into bite-sized pieces.

Char the Corn:

1. Heat a grill pan or skillet over medium-high heat. Add corn kernels in a single layer and cook, stirring occasionally, until charred in spots, about 5-7 minutes. Remove from heat and set aside.

Prepare Ramen Noodles:

1. In a large pot, bring water to a boil and cook the ramen noodles according to the package instructions. Drain and rinse under cold water to stop cooking. Divide the noodles among serving bowls.

Make the Ramen Broth:

1. In the same pot used for noodles (or a separate pot if needed), heat vegetable oil over medium heat. Add minced garlic and grated ginger, sauté for 1-2 minutes until fragrant.

2. Pour in chicken broth, soy sauce, and sesame oil. Bring to a simmer and let it cook for about 5 minutes to allow the flavors to meld together. Taste and adjust seasoning with soy sauce or salt if needed.

Assemble the Ramen Bowls:

1. Divide the cooked ramen noodles among serving bowls.
2. Ladle the hot broth over the noodles.
3. Add cooked chicken pieces and charred corn to each bowl.

Garnish and Serve:

1. Garnish each bowl with chopped green onions and sesame seeds.
2. Add optional toppings like sliced bamboo shoots, baby bok choy, or soft-boiled eggs if desired.

Enjoy! Serve hot and enjoy your delicious Chicken Ramen with Charred Corn! This recipe serves 2-4 people depending on portion sizes. Adjust the ingredients accordingly for larger servings. It's a comforting and flavorful ramen dish that combines the sweetness of charred corn with the savory richness of chicken and soy-infused broth.

Pork Ramen with Ramson Pesto

Ingredients:

For the Pork:

- 1 lb pork shoulder or pork belly, thinly sliced
- Salt and pepper, to taste
- 1 tbsp vegetable oil

For the Ramen:

- 2 packs of ramen noodles (discard seasoning packets)
- 6 cups pork or chicken broth
- 1 cup ramson leaves (wild garlic), washed and chopped
- 4 cloves garlic, minced
- 1-inch piece of ginger, grated
- 2 tbsp soy sauce
- 1 tbsp sesame oil
- 1 tbsp vegetable oil
- 2 green onions, chopped (white and green parts separated)
- Optional: soft-boiled egg, bamboo shoots, nori (seaweed), sesame seeds

Instructions:

Prepare the Pork:

1. Season pork slices with salt and pepper.
2. Heat vegetable oil in a large skillet or pan over medium-high heat. Add pork slices and cook until browned and cooked through, about 2-3 minutes per side. Remove from skillet and set aside.

Prepare Ramen Noodles:

1. In a large pot, bring water to a boil and cook the ramen noodles according to the package instructions. Drain and rinse under cold water to stop cooking. Divide the noodles among serving bowls.

Make the Ramson Pesto:

1. In a food processor or blender, combine ramson leaves, minced garlic, grated ginger, soy sauce, sesame oil, and vegetable oil. Blend until smooth, adding a little water if needed to achieve a pesto-like consistency.

Make the Ramen Broth:

1. In the same pot used for noodles (or a separate pot if needed), heat vegetable oil over medium heat. Add minced garlic and grated ginger, sauté for 1-2 minutes until fragrant.
2. Pour in pork or chicken broth and bring to a simmer.

3. Stir in the ramson pesto and let it simmer for about 5 minutes to allow the flavors to meld together. Taste and adjust seasoning with soy sauce or salt if needed.

Assemble the Ramen Bowls:

1. Divide the cooked ramen noodles among serving bowls.
2. Ladle the hot ramson pesto broth over the noodles.
3. Add cooked pork slices to each bowl.

Garnish and Serve:

1. Garnish each bowl with chopped green onions and optional toppings like a soft-boiled egg, bamboo shoots, nori, and sesame seeds.

Enjoy! Serve hot and enjoy your unique Pork Ramen with Ramson Pesto! This recipe serves 2-4 people depending on portion sizes. Adjust the ingredients accordingly for larger servings. It's a flavorful and aromatic ramen dish that highlights the seasonal freshness of ramsons with tender pork and savory broth.

Duck Ramen with Five-Spice Powder

Ingredients:

For the Duck:

- 2 duck breasts
- Salt and pepper, to taste
- 1 tbsp five-spice powder
- 1 tbsp vegetable oil

For the Ramen:

- 2 packs of ramen noodles (discard seasoning packets)
- 6 cups chicken or duck broth
- 4 cloves garlic, minced
- 1-inch piece of ginger, grated
- 2 tbsp soy sauce
- 1 tbsp mirin
- 1 tbsp sesame oil
- 1 tbsp vegetable oil
- 2 green onions, chopped (white and green parts separated)
- Optional: baby bok choy, bamboo shoots, soft-boiled egg
- Sesame seeds, for garnish

Instructions:

Prepare the Duck:

1. Score the skin of the duck breasts with a sharp knife in a crisscross pattern. This helps to render the fat and crisp up the skin.
2. Season both sides of the duck breasts with salt, pepper, and five-spice powder.
3. Heat vegetable oil in a large skillet or pan over medium-high heat. Place the duck breasts skin-side down and cook for about 5-6 minutes, until the skin is crispy and golden brown. Flip and cook for another 3-4 minutes for medium-rare, or longer to desired doneness. Remove from heat and let rest for a few minutes before slicing thinly.

Prepare Ramen Noodles:

1. In a large pot, bring water to a boil and cook the ramen noodles according to the package instructions. Drain and rinse under cold water to stop cooking. Divide the noodles among serving bowls.

Make the Ramen Broth:

1. In the same pot used for noodles (or a separate pot if needed), heat vegetable oil over medium heat. Add minced garlic and grated ginger, sauté for 1-2 minutes until fragrant.
2. Pour in chicken or duck broth, soy sauce, mirin, and sesame oil. Bring to a simmer and let it cook for about 5 minutes to allow the flavors to meld together. Taste and adjust seasoning with soy sauce or salt if needed.

Assemble the Ramen Bowls:

1. Divide the cooked ramen noodles among serving bowls.
2. Ladle the hot broth over the noodles.
3. Add sliced duck breast pieces to each bowl.

Garnish and Serve:

1. Garnish each bowl with chopped green onions and sesame seeds.
2. Add optional toppings like baby bok choy, bamboo shoots, or a soft-boiled egg if desired.

Enjoy! Serve hot and enjoy your delicious Duck Ramen with Five-Spice Powder! This recipe serves 2-4 people depending on portion sizes. Adjust the ingredients accordingly for larger servings. It's a decadent and flavorful ramen dish that highlights the unique taste of duck enhanced by aromatic five-spice powder in a comforting broth.

Beef Ramen with Caramelized Onions

Ingredients:

For the Beef:

- 1 lb beef sirloin or flank steak, thinly sliced
- Salt and pepper, to taste
- 1 tbsp vegetable oil

For the Caramelized Onions:

- 2 large onions, thinly sliced
- 2 tbsp unsalted butter
- 1 tbsp vegetable oil
- Pinch of salt

For the Ramen:

- 2 packs of ramen noodles (discard seasoning packets)
- 6 cups beef broth
- 4 cloves garlic, minced
- 1-inch piece of ginger, grated
- 2 tbsp soy sauce
- 1 tbsp mirin (Japanese rice wine) or rice vinegar
- 1 tbsp sesame oil
- 1 tbsp vegetable oil
- 2 green onions, chopped (white and green parts separated)
- Optional: soft-boiled egg, sliced bamboo shoots, nori (seaweed), sesame seeds

Instructions:

Prepare the Caramelized Onions:

1. Heat butter and vegetable oil in a large skillet over medium-low heat.
2. Add thinly sliced onions and a pinch of salt. Cook, stirring occasionally, until onions are deeply golden brown and caramelized, about 30-40 minutes. Stir occasionally to prevent burning. Set aside.

Prepare the Beef:

1. Season beef slices with salt and pepper.
2. Heat vegetable oil in a large skillet or pan over medium-high heat. Add beef slices and cook until browned and cooked through, about 2-3 minutes per side. Remove from skillet and set aside.

Prepare Ramen Noodles:

1. In a large pot, bring water to a boil and cook the ramen noodles according to the package instructions. Drain and rinse under cold water to stop cooking. Divide the noodles among serving bowls.

Make the Ramen Broth:

1. In the same pot used for noodles (or a separate pot if needed), heat vegetable oil over medium heat. Add minced garlic and grated ginger, sauté for 1-2 minutes until fragrant.
2. Pour in beef broth, soy sauce, mirin (or rice vinegar), and sesame oil. Bring to a simmer and let it cook for about 5 minutes to allow the flavors to meld together. Taste and adjust seasoning with soy sauce or salt if needed.

Assemble the Ramen Bowls:

1. Divide the cooked ramen noodles among serving bowls.
2. Ladle the hot broth over the noodles.
3. Add cooked beef slices and a generous portion of caramelized onions to each bowl.

Garnish and Serve:

1. Garnish each bowl with chopped green onions and optional toppings like a soft-boiled egg, sliced bamboo shoots, nori, and sesame seeds.

Enjoy! Serve hot and enjoy your delicious Beef Ramen with Caramelized Onions! This recipe serves 2-4 people depending on portion sizes. Adjust the ingredients accordingly for larger servings. It's a comforting and savory ramen dish that combines tender beef, sweet caramelized onions, and a rich broth flavored with soy and sesame.

Chicken Ramen with Lemongrass and Galangal

Ingredients:

For the Chicken:

- 2 boneless, skinless chicken breasts
- Salt and pepper, to taste
- 1 tbsp vegetable oil

For the Ramen:

- 2 packs of ramen noodles (discard seasoning packets)
- 6 cups chicken broth
- 2 stalks lemongrass, tough outer layers removed, smashed and chopped into pieces
- 1-inch piece of galangal, sliced (can substitute with ginger if unavailable)
- 4 cloves garlic, minced
- 2 tbsp soy sauce
- 1 tbsp fish sauce
- 1 tbsp lime juice
- 1 tbsp vegetable oil
- 2 green onions, chopped (white and green parts separated)
- Optional: sliced bamboo shoots, baby bok choy, cilantro leaves, Thai basil leaves, lime wedges

Instructions:

Prepare the Chicken:

1. Season chicken breasts with salt and pepper on both sides.
2. Heat vegetable oil in a large skillet or pan over medium-high heat. Add chicken breasts and cook for about 6-7 minutes per side, or until fully cooked and internal temperature reaches 165°F (74°C). Remove from heat, let rest for a few minutes, then slice or shred into bite-sized pieces.

Prepare Ramen Noodles:

1. In a large pot, bring water to a boil and cook the ramen noodles according to the package instructions. Drain and rinse under cold water to stop cooking. Divide the noodles among serving bowls.

Make the Lemongrass and Galangal Broth:

1. In the same pot used for noodles (or a separate pot if needed), heat vegetable oil over medium heat. Add minced garlic, chopped lemongrass, and sliced galangal. Sauté for 1-2 minutes until fragrant.
2. Pour in chicken broth, soy sauce, fish sauce, and lime juice. Bring to a simmer and let it cook for about 10-15 minutes to allow the flavors to meld together and the broth to infuse with lemongrass and galangal flavors. Taste and adjust seasoning with soy sauce, fish sauce, or lime juice if needed.

Assemble the Ramen Bowls:

1. Divide the cooked ramen noodles among serving bowls.
2. Ladle the hot lemongrass and galangal broth over the noodles.
3. Add cooked chicken pieces to each bowl.

Garnish and Serve:

1. Garnish each bowl with chopped green onions, and optional toppings like sliced bamboo shoots, baby bok choy, cilantro leaves, Thai basil leaves, and lime wedges.

Enjoy! Serve hot and enjoy your delicious Chicken Ramen with Lemongrass and Galangal! This recipe serves 2-4 people depending on portion sizes. Adjust the ingredients accordingly for larger servings. It's a refreshing and aromatic ramen dish that combines the bright flavors of lemongrass and galangal with tender chicken and a savory broth, perfect for a comforting meal.

Vegetarian Ramen with Crispy Shallots

Ingredients:

For the Crispy Shallots:

- 4-5 shallots, thinly sliced

- Vegetable oil for frying
- Pinch of salt

For the Ramen:

- 2 packs of ramen noodles (discard seasoning packets)
- 6 cups vegetable broth
- 4 cloves garlic, minced
- 1-inch piece of ginger, grated
- 2 tbsp soy sauce (or tamari for gluten-free option)
- 1 tbsp miso paste
- 1 tbsp sesame oil
- 1 tbsp vegetable oil
- 2 green onions, chopped (white and green parts separated)
- Optional: sliced bamboo shoots, baby bok choy, tofu cubes, nori (seaweed), sesame seeds

Instructions:

Prepare the Crispy Shallots:

1. Heat vegetable oil in a small skillet or pan over medium-high heat.
2. Add thinly sliced shallots to the hot oil, spreading them out into a single layer. Fry until golden brown and crispy, stirring occasionally, about 5-7 minutes. Watch closely to prevent burning.
3. Remove crispy shallots with a slotted spoon and transfer to a paper towel-lined plate. Sprinkle with a pinch of salt while still hot. Set aside.

Prepare Ramen Noodles:

1. In a large pot, bring water to a boil and cook the ramen noodles according to the package instructions. Drain and rinse under cold water to stop cooking. Divide the noodles among serving bowls.

Make the Ramen Broth:

1. In the same pot used for noodles (or a separate pot if needed), heat vegetable oil over medium heat. Add minced garlic and grated ginger, sauté for 1-2 minutes until fragrant.
2. Pour in vegetable broth and bring to a simmer.
3. Stir in soy sauce (or tamari), miso paste, and sesame oil. Simmer for about 5 minutes to allow the flavors to meld together. Taste and adjust seasoning with soy sauce or miso paste if needed.

Assemble the Ramen Bowls:

1. Divide the cooked ramen noodles among serving bowls.

2. Ladle the hot broth over the noodles.
3. Add optional toppings such as sliced bamboo shoots, baby bok choy, tofu cubes, and green onions.

Garnish and Serve:

1. Garnish each bowl with crispy shallots, chopped green onions, and any additional toppings like nori and sesame seeds.

Enjoy! Serve hot and enjoy your delicious Vegetarian Ramen with Crispy Shallots! This recipe serves 2-4 people depending on portion sizes. Adjust the ingredients accordingly for larger servings. It's a flavorful and satisfying ramen dish that combines the umami richness of miso with the crunch of crispy shallots, perfect for a comforting and hearty meal.

www.ingramcontent.com/pod-product-compliance
Lightning Source LLC
LaVergne TN
LVHW081601060526
838201LV00054B/2009